MARCO

Travel with
Insider
Tips

SICILY

AUSTRIA
CH
HUNG.
Milan Verona SLOVENIA
ITALY CROATIA
BOSN. &
MC SAN HERZEG.
MARINO SERBIA
Corsica MNE RKS
(F) Rome
MAC.
Naples
Sardinia ALBANIA
(I) Capri
Mediterranean
Sea
Palermo
Sicily

The best Insider Tips → p. 4

INSIDER TIP

Best of ... → p. 6

The Northeast → p. 32

The Southeast → p. 46

SYMBOLS

INSIDER TIP   Insider Tip

★   Highlight

●●●●   Best of ...

☼   Scenic view

☺   Responsible travel: for ecological or fair trade aspects

(*)   Telephone numbers that
are not toll-free

**PRICE CATEGORIES
HOTELS**

Expensive   over 120 euros

Moderate   80–120 euros

Budget   under 80 euros

Price for a double room
with breakfast in the high
season (except 1–20 August)
per night

**PRICE CATEGORIES
RESTAURANTS**

Expensive   over 50 euros

Moderate   30–50 euros

Budget   under 30 euros

Prices for a meal with a start-
er, main course and dessert,
but without drinks

On the cover: Fiery night sky over Stromboli p. 92 | Rural retreats p. 17, 116

CONTENTS

The North Coast → p. 60

The Southwest → p. 72

The Aeolian Islands → p. 86

Road atlas → p. 126

MAPS IN THE GUIDEBOOK
(128 A1) Page numbers and coordinates refer to the road atlas
(0) Site/address located off the map. Coordinates are also given for places that are not marked on the road atlas
Street maps of Catania, Palermo, Taormina and Trapani inside the back cover
Street map of Syracuse → p. 56

INSIDE BACK COVER: PULL-OUT MAP →

PULL-OUT MAP 📖
(📖 A–B 2–3) Refers to the removable pull-out map

The best MARCO POLO Insider Tips

Our top 15 Insider Tips

INSIDER TIP **Devils and Co.**
On Good Friday in San Fratello, villains in red with masks and tin drums take to the streets and interrupt the processions. Priests and the police take no notice – and the crowds love it → **p. 110, 113**

INSIDER TIP **Catania's elegant bars**
The *tavola calda* in the bar Etoile d'Or is a treasure not to be missed → **p. 36**

INSIDER TIP **Pure bliss**
In Vendicari Nature Reserve you can watch flamingos, herons and storks from close up, walk for miles along empty beaches without seeing anyone and explore a holiday paradise between sandbanks and lagoons (photo above) → **p. 53**

INSIDER TIP **China made in Sicily**
Building work and the decoration of the Palazzina Cinese in Palermo was done exclusively by Italians → **p. 67**

INSIDER TIP **The impregnable**
Sheer cliff faces, several defence walls and just one steep approach with heavily fortified gates made the Rocca di Cefalù impregnable. Paths now lead up to the top of the 268m (880ft) high rock above Cefalù although the best view of the Old Town and the cathedral is half way up (photo right) → **p. 62**

INSIDER TIP **Lots of sand all to yourself**
Dunes, woods, fine sand, clear water and few people make the beaches between Sciacca and Montallegro the perfect place to enjoy a peaceful day sunbathing, swimming or snorkelling → **p. 81**

INSIDER TIP **A hidden paradise**
The lush green Gardens of the Kolymbetra are hidden below the temples in Agrigento and cult sites of earthly gods. Their almond and orange trees have turned this into a true Garden of Eden → **p. 75**

BEST OF ...

GREAT PLACES FOR FREE
Discover new places and save money

● *From stronghold to museum*
The medieval *Castello Ursino* has survived earthquakes, battles and lava flows from Etna. Inside the sturdy fortress you can step back into the past and marvel at the archeological finds, antique coins and paintings for free → p. 35

● *Tea-time*
You can find out everything to do with tea in the *Casa-Museo del Tè* in Raddusa where the rooms are designed to Feng-Shui rules. Entrance is free and, if you want to do some good, you can buy a small souvenir and support one of the Casa's charity projects → p. 51

● *Open-air gallery*
Take a brisk walk rather than standing around: the *Fiumara d'Arte*, with its large sculptures that can be seen from some distance, a pyramid and a labyrinth, is located on the hills above the Messina–Palermo coast road → p. 63

● *Tapping the source*
Help yourself to mineral water directly from the spring – and free of charge – at the old fountain outside the mountain village of Geraci Siculo. Just take your own bottles to fill up and a bit of patience, as you'll have to wait your turn → p. 64

● *Wine, in theory and practice*
If coaches are parked outside *Enomuseo* in Marsala, then it's going to be a squash inside. Enjoy a fascinating look at the equipment needed to cultivate grapes and make wine, with a glass in your hand → p. 77

● *Column drums from Antiquity*
For some 2500 years, column drums intended for building temples in Selinunt have been lying in *Rocche di Cusa*. Treat yourself to a lovely free stroll through natural surroundings between rocks, large trees and impressive remains from Antiquity (photo) → p. 79

●●●● Dots in guidebook refer to 'Best of ...' tips

● *A cap with a history*

Once a symbol of the Mafia: the *coppola,* the Sicilian peaked cap made of hardwearing material. Fashion designers have now rediscovered it. You can even find them in velvet – or in white to go with a wedding dress. Whatever your taste, head for *La Coppola Storta* in Palermo → p. 69

● *Puppet shows*

Wild fights and loud kisses are both part of Sicilian marionette theatre performances, in which wooden figures play out the adventures of knights of old fighting the Saracens or come to the rescue of damsels in distress. Great fun – and not just for children → p. 33, 109

● *Intensive aromas*

Oregano and wild fennel make Sicilian dishes so tasty. The herbs used in local dishes on the Aeolian Islands produce the most intense aromas. Find out for yourself by sampling the traditional and delicious food in *Filippino* on Lipari or in *Punta Lena* on Stromboli → p. 89, 93

● *Veg to go*

The real *caponata* made of aubergines, celery, capers, green olives, wild fennel and tomatoes is eaten cold. Farmers take it with them to the fields. Try it at *Casale Villa Rainò* near Gangi where the country feel comes free of charge → p. 64

● *Ceramic works of art*

The Arabs left their mark on Sicilian art: dazzling blues, delicate yellows, a little red – typical colours of the ceramics found in Caltagirone, Sciacca and Burgio (photo). You'll find particularly bright colours along the main road in *St. Stefano di Camastra* → p. 63

● *Intoxicated by the colours and smells*

The street markets in Catania and Palermo with their colourful wares and bustling activity stimulate the senses. Immerse yourself in a world of artistically stacked fruit and vegetable pyramids, the variety of mysterious sea creatures on sale, the smell of fish and the scent of oranges. And even if you can't stomach the idea of a calf's foot decorated with myrtle twigs, then at least feast on the banquet with your eyes → p. 36, 69

BEST OF ...

● *Undersea world*
In Messina's aquarium you can come face to face with some of the creatures that live in the straits, including many that are otherwise out of sight in the depths of the sea → p. 40

● *Plates and bowls*
When it rains, the bright tiles on the walls of the ceramics museum in Caltagirone are especially lovely. Inside, the hundreds of tiles, vases, bowls, plates, jugs and figures from Antiquity are quite a sight – even when dry → p. 48

● *Archeology under cover*
The mosaics in the Late Roman *Villa del Casale* near Piazza Armerina cover 44,130ft² and have been roofed over. You can spend hours here in the ruins of this imperial villa (photo) → p. 50

● *Classicist opera house*
Even if you're not an opera fan you should still pay a visit to Palermo's *Teatro Massimo*. Italy's largest opera house includes magnificent decorations from the turn-of-the-century that you can marvel at in silence when the orchestra pit and stage are empty → p. 68

● *Tale-telling columns*
The cloister in Monreale was like a golden cage in which the 228 capitals of the columns told monks tales of kings and saints, of dragons and man-eating monsters. A tip: when it's raining, the light is ideal for taking photographs → p. 71

● *Off to the spa*
Soak in the 38° C (100° F) warm spa water in *Terme Segestane* and you'll never notice that it's raining! Pure bliss in the evening after a long outing → p. 85

RAIN

RELAX AND CHILL OUT
Take it easy and spoil yourself

● *Seeking refuge higher up*

In the stone-built *Agriturismo Cirasella* in Sant'Alfio, almost 3300ft above sea level, you can enjoy the peace of a country holiday with just the sound of the birds below tall trees on the flanks of Mount Etna, and tuck into the excellent organic food produced on the farm → **p. 34**

● *Mountaineering made easy*

If you're not a keen hiker, then take a trip in the cable car up Etna (from the end of the road at Rifugio Sapienza) and soak up the magnificent views. For the remaining 9500ft you can take a tour in an off-road minibus → **p. 37**

● *Boat trip through beautiful scenery*

Sit back and enjoy a boat trip on the narrow, cool River Ciane south of Syracuse and marvel at the dense vegetation along the banks of reeds, couch grass and papyrus (photo) → **p. 59**

● *Oasis in the metropolis*

Stop off at the botanic garden in Palermo after a sightseeing trip – get away from the traffic and the noise of the city. Lying on a park bench under tropical trees and watching the rose-ringed parakeets from Africa flying among the treetops is pure relaxation → **p. 67**

● *An island of peace*

For those who really want to turn their backs on things, just take a boat from Salina to *Alicudi* and soak up the silence which is like nothing you'll ever have experienced before. A small harbour, a hotel and restaurant, a few houses on the main path to the top of the volcano – that's all there is on the island. Even the most active of people adopt a slower pace of life here → **p. 92**

● *Water massage*

Warm spring water fills the large pool in the *Terme di Acqua* Pia near Gibellina and you can experience its gentle power sitting under one of the waterfalls. Or else you spoil yourself with a health and beauty therapy → **p. 79**

INTRODUCTION

DISCOVER SICILY!

'Araaaance, arance fresche dell'Etna!' Carmine the market crier's singsong echoes through the Baroque streets of Palermo's Old Town with its flaking façades – a long drawn out falsetto like a plaintive Arab melody. Shutters are thrown open; widows dressed in black appear on balconies where canaries are kept in their cages. They lower their *paniere* – their wicker shopping baskets – on long ropes. The 'Ape Piaggo' three-wheeler van, with its colourful rusty patches, is piled high with blood oranges. The scent of the citrus fruit's leaves in the blazing summer heat mingles with the smell of swordfish in garlic from a *trattoria* with bright flourescent lights and a flickering television. *Sicilia eterna* – the slow-paced 'eternal' Sicily of old really does still exist. But anyone who thinks that the few confusingly chaotic districts in the Old Town or the intoxicating hustle-and-bustle of the fish market are the real Sicily, is definitely behind the times.

Young girls in tight jeans with jet-black hair down to their waists, sounding their horns as they charge around on their Vespas with their 'Mafia: no grazie' stickers, are neither

Photo: View towards Etna

More than 2,400 years old – the Temple of Concorde in the Valle dei Templi near Agrigento

'hot trophies' nor 'token women', but simply part of everyday life. Their grandmothers, the older generation of *nonna*, used to be more hesitant about being out on the street, except when they went to church. An active lifestyle with cycling and hiking *(escursionismo)* has suddenly become hip among young Sicilians. Local groups put their new trekking shoes to the test in the *Riserva dello Zingaro* nature reserve in the far northeast, where their walks take them past abandoned tuna fisheries, swathes of yellow surge and turquoise bays. Renovated farms, now run as *agriturismi,* attract Italians from the north tired of the rat race as well as other Europeans who are into organic living. *Nero d'Avola* has turned into the local cult wine and top wine-makers refine the taste by completing the ripening process in clay amphoras.

> **Young Sicilians find cycling and hiking hip**

800–580 BC
Founding of many Phoenician and Greek towns around the coast of Sicily

241 BC–440 AD
Sicily becomes a Roman province after the First Punic War and remains so for 700 years

827–1061
Sicily under Arab rule; Palermo becomes the capital city in 901

1061–91
Sicily is conquered by the Normans. A refined culture emerges during the 150 years under the Normans and the House of Hohenstaufen that combines Arabic, Byzantine and European traditions

In the one real tourist hotspot on the island, in Taormina with its view of Etna photographed millions of times, five-star luxury hotels are sprouting up all over the place like during the Belle Epoque. Solvent guests frequently include weekend visitors from larger cities, whereas during the lively and loud *movida* that rampages through Catania's lavic stone *centro storico* on balmy summer evenings, there are few holiday-makers to be found. Celebrations are more boisterous here than in the melancholic metropolis of Palermo. Provincial towns such as Comiso or Acireale have a surprising number of elegant boutiques. The typical man on Sicily today is dressed in a dark suit and tie – or else in a pink T-shirt as a *tifoso* of Palermo Calcio. For the first time in decades, a Sicilian football team is at last back in the first division.

The old picture of the hard-done-by south, always seeing itself as the exploited victim with little much to offer other than organised crime, a declining population and poverty, is a picture that no longer applies. *Vittimismo* as a frame of mind is now *passé*.

> **The south is no longer a region left out in the cold**

Even the all-pavading Mafia has mutated into an economic driving force and an attraction for cineastes. Since the province of Palermo has been promoting its image at travel and tourism fairs with companies that refuse to pay the *pizzo* (protection money), the threat has boosted tourism: 'We are anti Mafia' has turned into a tourist experience. The flat cap worn by tanned farm-workers and Sicilian gangsters has returned as a cheekily striped piece of Hollywood headgear. Even the *baristas* at the aiport wear their *coppola* with charming nonchalance.

1266
After the death of the Staufen king Frederick II, the Pope puts the French Anjou famiiy on the throne of Sicily

1282–1700
Sicily comes under the rule of the Spanish crown

1734–1860
Under the rule of the Bourbons who also command Naples

1860
The conquest of Sicily by Garibaldi marks the start of the Unification of Italy

ca. 1870
The wave of emigration to America starts; ten years later the Mafia and organised crime take hold

Sicilia est insula: this truism drummed into the heads of Latin pupils conceals more than first meets the eye. Covering 25,709km² (9927mi²) it is the largest island in the Mediterranean – and a very special one at that. It is closer to Libya and Tunisia than to Milan. And it is too powerful, too culturally important, too modern to pretend to be a mere provincial, Mediterranean outpost. The Ancient Greeks performed their first improvised comedies in Syracuse while the temples in Agrigento continue to provide a fascinating display of harmonious proportion. Whereas Italian once evolved into the language of literature at royal courts in central Europe, computer programmers and software engineers in Etna Valley today have long since had to come to grips with the niceties of English. After years of neglect, the Art Nouveau Teatro Massimo in Palermo resounds once again to the sound of Bellini, Wagner and Puccini. Star chefs from Trapani or Ragusa jet back and forth to Tokyo to let the Japanese in on the secrets of the *cucina siciliana* while TV cookery shows enthuse about the *cassata siciliana*'s Islamic roots and young Sicilians flirt quite openly with their oriental cultural heritage – 'Arab revival' is what they call it now. In the long term, the political upheaval in Maghreb will also provide Sicily with new possibilities. The fishing centre and port of Mazara del Vallo would long since have stopped trading were it not for workers from Tunisia.

> **The largest island in the Mediterranean is closer to Tunisia than Milan**

Un ponte sullo stretto – even without the controversial bridge across the strait between Messina and Reggio di Calabria that is to be completed by 2016, the more than 5 million Sicilians have been drawing ever closer to the rest of Europe. They have long become well integrated throughout mainland Italy as judges and poets, car mechanics and publicans, *carabinieri* and film directors. And yet Sicily still sometimes seems like a continent unto itself, running at a different pace and according to different rules. Even the colours are different. Everything somehow seems more intense. Nowhere else are the cherry trees and prickly pears, the cucumbers and aubergines as bright and shiny. In no other operatic performance is the public so vociferous as during *Cavalleria Rusticana*. Where else does the baleful music of Easter processions echo more sullenly through the mountain villages or do children, dressed as nuns and monks, drag along behind the decorated carts marking the Passion the evening before Good Friday? The Spanish and the Greeks, the Albanians and French, Normans and North

1943–47
Mafia terror against land reform, the black market and separatists almost plunge Sicily into civil war

Since 1975
The Mafia blatantly terrorises the state. Resistance is slow to form. In 1993, the 'Boss of Bosses', Totò Riina, is arrested, followed by his successor, Bernardo Provenzano, in 2006 and, later, by almost all bosses

2010
Construction of the bridge across the Strait of Messina starts

2016
Projected inauguration of the bridge

The Church's authority turned into stone: the architectural delights of Palermo Cathedral

Africans have all left their mark in the form of fortresses and cathedrals, sagas and culinary delights, music and facial features. The island has been multicultural for thousands for years to which the mass of historical sights testify.

The luxuriant cascades of bougainvillea, the spikey orange cactus fruit and the silvery-grey olive and knarled carob trees of the coastal regions provide a stark contrast to the sulphury, seemingly uninhabited countryside further inland with its

> **Sicilians love deep discussions and celebrations with friends**

waving fields of corn, overgrown paths, flocks of sheep and the *macchia*. The variety of beaches is also quite considerable, ranging from fine sand along the north coast, such as the one framing the fishing town of Cefalù at the foot of the limestone Madonie mountains, to pebbly lava beaches on the Aeolian island of Lipari. With blue grottoes below Taormina and the Gola d'Alcantara volcanic gorge, all the delights of the south are concentrated on Sicily.

Sicilians like being together with friends or engrossed in conversation, and – like Andrea Camilleri's Inspector Montalbano – enjoy hour-long feasts. *La bella figura*, extravagant tips, demonstrative idleness and tireless commentaries and appraisals with erotic undertones are eternal traits of the Sicilian way of life, as is the exuberant joy at meeting new people – demonstrated sometimes just a little bit too fast. The friend that Carmine the orange seller wanted to photograph suddenly finds herself surrounded by a number of other photo models – 'anche a me', 'why not me as well,' says Rosario, the gaunt owner of the trattoria opposite, as he forces himself into the picture, proudly holding up a tray of *cannoli* filled with fruit and ricotta …

WHAT'S HOT

1 Slowly does it

Travelling back in time In Sant'Ambrogio the cheese is carefully made by hand by Giulio the shepherd *(photo)* and the
dough left to rise naturally. The village has rediscovered
its traditional roots thanks to Carmelina Ricciardello, the
founder of the *Sicilian Experience*, who managed to convince
the locals of the benefits. Visitors profit from this
project that is more than a mere fad. *(Information and guided tours: Discesa Decano
Martino 10, Sant'Ambrogio, www.sicilian
experience.com).*

Natural beauty

2

Looking lovely Salt, olive oil and lemons: local
products are put to good use in the spa in the
Kempinski Hotel Giardino di Costanza Einsatz *(Via
Salemi km 7, Mazara del Vallo, photo)*. Beauty experts
in the *Belli Resort* also have faith in the benefits of
home-grown natural products and offer relaxing
therapies with essential pine oil, renowned Sicilian
salt and flower essence *(Via Roma 58/60, Gratteri)*.
Local delicacies such as organic honey and wine are good-
feel factors in the spa in *Hotel Biancaneve (Via Etnea 163,
Nicolosi)*.

3 Highlife on the beach

Night and day The beach clubs are only empty in the mornings when
clearing up after the previous night is underway. The cool
clubs acts as a magnet however long before sunset.
Paradise Beach Club starts off as a relaxing lounge
bar then becomes an elegant restaurant before
turning into a disco after dark *(Via Luigi Rizzo,
Letoianni, photo)*. Its party-time in trendy
Panasia Beach (Via Nazionale, Spisone) and
*Mendolina Beach Club (Via Nazionale 198,
Mazzarò)* as well, both night and day.

Eco-friendly accommodation

4

Where the lemon trees blossom In southern Italy, countryside and environmental issues are largely the domain of *agriturismo* farms. Organic is spellt with a captial 'O' on the lemon farm *Limoneto*, both in the groves and in the kitchen where you can sample the delights of the Sicilian cuisine *(Via del Platano 3, Syracuse, www.limoneto.it, photo)*. Cooking on solar power and showing with rainwater: the emphasis at *Etnalodge* is not only on environmental protection but courses and workshops are also held on how to save energy at home *(Via Bassi 21, Piedimonte Etneo, www.etnalodge.it)*. Not only the walls at *Agriturismo Guarnera* are painted with the environment is mind, the pool is fitted out with a natural chlorine-free filtration system *(Contrada Gargi di Cenere, Cefalù, www.gargidicenere.it)*.

Old & new

5

The joys of art Sicily is rich in history and works of art. And there is also a young and expanding art scene on the island. One of the trailblazers is Francesco Pantaleone who runs a contemporary art gallery in Palermo's *Palazzo Nobile (Via Garraffello 25, www.fpac.it)*. The *Museum Riso* has more space for displaying paintings, photographs and sculpture *(Museo d'Arte Contemporanea della Sicilia, Corso Vittorio Emanuele 365, Palermo, www.palazzoriso.it)*. Modern art is not just for looking at, you can live in it too, such as in Rocco Forte's stylishly designed *Verdura Golf & Spa Resort* on the south coast *(Sciacca, www.verduraresort.com, photo)*.

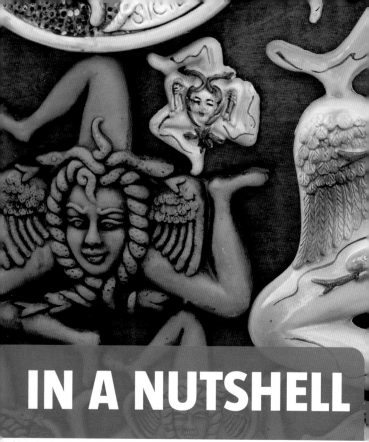

IN A NUTSHELL

BRIDGING THE GAP

The Messina Strait Bridge is expected to be completed in 2016. The suspension bridge will be 3.3km (2mi) long, the two towers 382m (1.253ft) high, and the carriageway 50–65m (165–213ft) above the sea. The cost is estimated as 6.3 billion euros. Critics point out the high risks posed by storms and earthquakes and the exaggerated scale of the project. It is being built to cope with 200 trains and 140,000 cars crossing the bridge every day.

THE CHURCH

Apart from the Albanians and the growing number of Tunisians and Moroccans, practically all Sicilians are Catholic. The Church still has a strong influence on virtually all aspects of everyday life and always makes itself heard, even if it has to apply a little pressure. The majority of kindergartens and a lot of schools are in the hands of the Church, as are many social institutions. The influence of nuns on children and mothers is widespread even if the involvement of the Church is only apparent outwardly. Marrying in white and a church funeral are a matter of course; regular church attendance less so. Women are definitely more active in this respect – with this involvement increasing with age. Fundamental church groups, priests, mem-

Photo: The *trinacria* – the emblem of Sicily

Addio pizzo, benvenuti coppola: the Mafia and hip headgear, concrete hideosities and organic fare, the Church and the *corso* on Sicily

bers of religious orders and church dignitaries are working more and more for changes. Answers to the problem of the Mafia and people's fear of it, building and land speculation, corruption in politics, the decimation of the environment, spiralling drug addiction and petty criminality in urban centres, unemployment and a renewed increase in illiteracy, are often sought in the Church.

COPPOLA & CO.

The *coppola*, the flat cap, now enjoys cult status and is a fashionable expression of *sicilianità* – quite independent of a person's social status. It used to be common for men in the country to wear flat caps as it indicated that they were tenant farmers, agricultural workers, peasants or shepherds. More sturdy hats with a wider brim were reserved for the rural and provincial

This pilgrim church is dedicated to Saint Rosalia, the patron saint of Palermo

bourgeoisie and the nobility. The *coppola* got a bad name through its association with the Mafia as it was largely worn by the big bosses' right-hand men. But in the meanwhile even Hollywood stars like Brad Pitt can be seen in a *coppola*. And a leading Sicilian hat-maker has opened up shops in New York and Berlin *(www.lacoppola storta.it)*.

EMIGRATION

Millions of Sicilians, equalling almost the entire population increase over the past 120 years, emigrated abroad – mainly to the USA. After World War II they headed for the industrial centres in western Europe and northern Italy. Poverty and the lack of perspectives drove the rural population in particular away from their native country. The annexation of Sicily and the unification of Italy in 1860 did not result in a land reform or an improvement in the social status of tenant farmers, day labourers and agricultural workers. The work of crafts people was swiftly ruined by the import of industrial products from northern Italy and elsewhere, and Sicily's most important industry, sulphur mining, came virtually to a standstill due to competition from America where it was produced much more cheaply.

Sicilian colonies flourished in the large urban centres in America and – just like back home – the Mafia and other underground organisations with criminal objectives soon became the driving forces. Today, emigration is hardly an issue despite the depressingly high unemployment rate among young people in particular.

ENVIRONMENTAL ISSUES

Even travellers in the 18th century commented on the rubbish in Palermo. Since time immemorial Sicilians have treated the environment with typical Mediterranean *laissez-faire*. Industrial ruins, concrete eyesores and (although decreasing in number) illegal dumps are the downside of *bella Sicilia*.

However there has been a noticeable re-think. The Regional Agency for the Protection of the Environment (ARPA) campaigns in schools, boats patrol the coasts to make sure there is no illegal building work. The regional parks and more than 50 conservation areas are visited by enthusiastic local hikers or *escursionisti*.

Mangiare sano: the considerable value now placed on health food has resulted in Italian's sun-blessed island becoming the biggest supplier of organic products. The younger generation is well aware as to how the economy of post-industrial Sicily can only benefit from an ecologically 'green' image. The number of *bandiera blu* beaches (with a blue flag for ecological awareness) still has to be expanded. The mass of fish in the markets rather hides the fact that tuna is acutely endangered – something, however, that is more due to fleets of sea-going vessels.

FAMILY LIFE

The extended family conditions the everyday routine, as has always been the case, even if there have been many changes over the past few years especially in the towns and among the younger generation – and not only now as a result of divorce becoming more common. The roles and tasks of each person in a family are set in concrete. Everything within a house is governed by the women, everything outside by the men. The most important woman in a man's life is not his wife or lover, but his own mother. She knows the secrets of homemade pasta and sauces, she is proud of her son, of his car, his house and his children.

GARIBALDI

Italy's national hero, Giuseppe Garibaldi, was born in 1807 in Nice. He was a member of an underground movement working for the unification of Italy, fled to France and South America in 1834 and returned to Italy in 1848. In the service of the House of Savoy he led his legion in unsuccessful exploits against Austria and the Papal States, to which large areas of northern and central Italy belonged at that time. Garibaldi left for America but later returned to Europe, setting up home on the island of Caprera off the coast of Sardinia. It was from here that he organised a thousand volunteers – *i Mille*, known as the 'Redshirts' – who landed at Marsala, Sicily, on 11 May, 1860 and defeated the Bourbon troups on 15 May at Calatafimi. He received support from all levels of society. Palermo capitulated on 6 June; Messina on 28 July. On 7 September he conquered Naples, the capital of the Kingdom of the Two Sicilies, and declared Victor Emanuel King of Italy on 26 October, 1860.

THE MAFIA

The honourable gentlemen, the God-fathers and their killers have a hand in virtually everything that has to do with power and money. Drugs and prostitution, endless streams of refugees and the extortion of protection money are just some of the more familiar criminal activities. A network of friendships with politicians and officials right up to the top opens up the path to big money for public contracts and subventions, creates minor posts and furthers major careers. The Mafia is a parallel state whose instruments of power include corruption, fear and murder. Whoever breaks the *omertà*, the pledge of secrecy, pays for it with his life. The internal power struggles are equally lethal, with most deaths coming from within the Mafia's own ranks whenever new bosses and families fight for their share.

The modern Mafia in major cities has long been operating on a global scale, networking both legal and criminal businesses especially in the road construction and the health industries, as well as in waste disposal. The annual turnover in 2005, for example, was estimated at 40 billion euros at least. Such capital is increasingly being invested in legal businesses, often in the form of hostile takeovers.

Those who bravely stand up to the Mafia still risk being killed. Murders are becoming increasingly brutal, not even stopping short of children. However, the success had in searching for the perpetrators and the severe sentences without reprieve, combined with the solidarity and increased self-confidence of the general public, have weakened the Mafia. And instead of sitting in silence for the rest of their lives in prison, many of the 'bosses' spill the beans. Confiscated property and the businesses of convicted bosses are made over to cooperatives and provide a glimmer of hope, helping to ease the state of permanent unemployment in the countryside. They produce pasta, oil, cheese and wine under the trademark 'Libera Terra' *(www.libera terra.it)*. The cooperatives themselves – more than 400 in total – have joined forces with hoteliers, traders, farmers, craftsmen and builders to form 'Addio Pizzo' and no longer pay protection money *(pizzo)*. The organisation cooperates closely with the anti-Mafia networks in all provinces in Sicily. A map with all addresses – largely in the city and province of Palermo – is available wherever you see the 'Addio Pizzo' sticker on the door or under *www.addio pizzo.org*. For Catania and the Etna region see *www.addiopizzocatania.org*.

OPERA DEI PUPI

Heads rolls, Saracens are split in two and princesses abducted. There's never a dull moment in Sicilian marionette theatres when Orlando or Reynald fight for the Cross or for Charlemagne. But even the *puparo*, the puppeteer, can get out of breath, as performing is hard physical work in these family-run businesses. The brightly-coloured figures can be up to 1½m (5ft) high. They are hand-carved and operated using iron rods. In the 1980s this form of folk art was in danger of disappearing due to dwindling audiences. In the meantime, however, even local school classes now visit the shows. Palermo, Acireale and Monreale are the principle centres on Sicily where shows are held *(p. 109)*. In 2008 the Opera dei Pupi was designated by Unesco as part of humanity's 'oral and intangible heritage'.

PASSEGGIATA

The *passeggiata* – the evening stroll – starts before the sun has set. Everyone seems to be on the move and the main thoroughfare, the *corso*, as well as the main square, the *piazza*, are turned into a stage for two hours, where people meet up and like 'to see and be seen' by friends and anyone around. Gossip and news are exchanged and rumours spread. The *passeggiata* is also the perfect, carefully monitored occasion for lovers to show their affection for one another. This is when many an engagement and marriage finds its beginnnings and even business deals settled.

SARACEN TOWERS

The sturdy, sometimes round, sometimes square towers are a feature of the Italian coastline and also of Sicily. The Saracens from north Africa arrived on the shores of all Christian countries around the Mediterranean in the 9th century in their ships, plundered and destroyed coastal settlements and fought their way into the heart of each country, killing the local populace or taking them back for the slave market. Well fortified towns, however, were seldom attacked. The towers were within sight of one another and warnings were given by lighting fires or firing canons.

TRINACRIA

The winged head of Medusa, from which three bent legs emerge, has been used as an emblem for Sicily since Antiquity, symbolising its triangular shape and its three ancient provinces, as well as being a symbol of the sun and of fertility. Sicily's emblem can be seen everywhere – on postcards and souvenirs, on market stalls, fishing boats and lorries, on pub and shop signs, as a trademark of a brewery in Messina, on stamps, flags, Internet sites and official letterheads.

VOLCANOES & EARTHQUAKES

Geologically speaking, most of Sicily was part of Africa. Only the north is part of the Eurasian Plate and is being pushed by the Aftican Plate which resulted in the formation of the mountain ranges in northern Sicily. Earthquakes are caused by tension and the sudden release of energy in the earth's crust. In 1693, a quake destroyed the whole of southern Sicily. In 1783 and 1908 the most devastating earthquakes ever recorded in Europe almost entirely destroyed Messina; in 1969 it hit Gibellina in the west and other settlements in Belice Valley.

Volcanoes often appear along the seams where cracks and faults cause chambers of magma – which rise from the molten centre of the earth – to form. Etna and Stromboli are the two most visibly active volcanoes on Sicily. For volcanologists, the islands of Lipari, Vulcano, Panarea and Pantelleria are still active, although their last eruptions were more than 100 years ago. The islands Salina, Filicudi, Alicudi, Ustica and Linosa are extinct volcanoes.

Off the coast of Sicily, deep under the sea, there is a lot more going on. In the very shallow waters to the south, which are rich fishing grounds, between Agrigento, Sciacca, Pantelleria and Linosa, fisher-

There are wonderufl views of the sea from the Riserva dello Zingaro nature reserve

man frequently find cooked fish in their haul whenever they see air bubbles rising. In 1831, lava and hot volcanic ash created a new island in the sea off Sciacca. The British, French and Russians all wanted it and even threatened the rulers in Naples and each other with war. But before it got that far, the island, Ferdinandea, disappeared after five months back into the sea.

Deep under the Tyrrhenian Sea, north of the Aeolian Islands, lies Europe's largest, active volcanoe, Marsili, that covers an area of more than 770mi² and rises to a height of some 3000m (9850ft). It is still relatively poorly researched. It is surrounded by a ring of craters including at least seven other active, underwater volcanoes and the Aeolian Islands above the water. Marsili is permanently under surveillance. It cannot be predicted if and when it will erupt or cause an undersea earthquake with a devastating tsunami. It could be today, tomorrow or in 100,000 years.

FOOD & DRINK

Forget the picture you have of typical Italian food, of spaghetti bolognese and *frittura*. **Sicilian cuisine is different. It's made up of the culinary delights enjoyed by all foreign rulers and their chefs who made the island their home for hundreds of years.**

The food is different on every part of the island. Fishermen and shepherds, farmers from the fertile plains and workers from the great expanse of inland Sicily all have different ingredients at hand. And the food of the gentry is different again from that of their staff. But what they do have in common is creativity, fantasy and a love of colour, as well as an ability to combine sweet, savoury, hot and sour things quite daringly which, in the hands of Sicilian cooks, are magically turned into delicious dishes. Fresh white bread, usually with sesame seeds in the oriental tradition, and pasta – the omnipresent pasta – are never missing. The Sicilians are even record-holders within Italy, consuming more than 100 kg of pasta per capita every year. The other main ingredients in traditional Sicilian food are as varied as an average market stall. Seafood and vegetables are essential; oregano and wild fennel, that can be found everywhere in Sicily, are used together with generous quantities of fresh mint from the garden and basil.

Seafood, pasta and vegetables are the common ingredients used – regardless of whether you're rich or poor

The Sicilians eat late, both at lunchtime and in the evening. And they like eating, especially in a restaurant. They also have a good time on a Sunday picnic in the woods, the mountains or on the beach. Eating is simple as is a pleasure spending a relaxing time with friends. A generous sandwich – *panino* – or something fried such as rice balls – *arancini* – or chickpea biscuits – *panelli* – soon fill you up.

Eating out in a restaurant normally starts with *antipasti*, small delicious appetisers which tempt the eye and tease the taste buds, and which Italians seldom skip. They include seafood, mushrooms, olives, cooked or marinated vegetables, local cheeses, hams and salami, and perhaps chilled melon or fresh figs.

The *primo piatto*, the first course, is almost always a noodle dish, but could equally

LOCAL SPECIALITIES

▶ **alici marinate** – marinaded anchovies with fresh mint

▶ **cannoli** – small, crisp pasta rolls with a creamy ricotta filling (photo left)

▶ **caponata** – sweet-and-sour aubergines served cold with tomatoes, olives, capers and herbs

▶ **cicorie selvatiche** – wild greens (e.g. dandelion, rocket, thistle, fennel), usually rather bitter and acerbic

▶ **coniglio al agrodolce** – sweet-and-sour marinaded rabbit

▶ **farsumagru** – large veal roulade (700–800 g) filled with meat, eggs, olives, breadcrumbs and herbs

▶ **insalata di arance** – fresh oranges with delicately-tasting onions and olive oil

▶ **insalata di mare** – seafood in an olive oil and lemon marinade (photo right)

▶ **maccheroni alla Norma** – homemade pasta with fresh tomato sauce, grilled slices of aubergine and fresh or smoked ricotta

▶ **maccu di fave** – broadbean purée with olive oil and wild herbs

▶ **olive fritte** – black olives braised with garlic and herbs

▶ **pani cunzatu** – farmhouse bread filled with tomatoes, capers, olives, grated cheese, oregano and olive oil

▶ **parmigiana di melanzane** – casserole with aubergines, tomatoes, Parmesan and mozzarella

▶ **pasta con finocchio e sarde** – pasta with wild fennel and fresh sardines

▶ **peperonata** – oven-baked peppers in oil and vinegar marinade

▶ **pesto alla trapanese** – red tomato sauce with roasted almonds

▶ **sarde a beccafico** – roulade filled with deboned sardines, (in Palermo) with breadcrumbs, sultanas and pine nuts baked in the oven, or (in the east) with breadcrumbs, Pecorino and anchovies cooked in a pan

▶ **spaghetti/risotto col nero di seppia** – spaghetti or risotto with octopus in its own ink

▶ **tagliatelle con ragù di maiale** – spicey hot tagliatelle with pork ragout

▶ **tonno alla marinara** – with onions, olives, capers and tuna braised in tomatoes

▶ **zuppa di pesce** – fish soup with 4–5 different types of fish, small squid and shrimps; sometimes also with mussels and scampi

well be risotto or a plate of *gnocchetti*, marble sized potato balls served with a light tomato sauce. *Cuscus alla trapanese*, the steamed wheat dish, is of north-African origin and is served with hot seafood.

The *secondo piatto* is the main course of seafood, meat or eggs. This is usually accompanied by a side dish *(contorno)* which has to be ordered separately, comprising a salad or cooked vegetables that are often eaten cold in Sicily. The Strait of Messina and the north coast between Cefalù and the Aeolian Islands are in summer the best fishing grounds in Italy for swordfish. Its lean meat is cooked on a charcoal grill, steamed with sweet tomatoes, capers and herbs or served with an olive oil, lemon, garlic and oregano sauce *(pesce spada al sammurighiu)*. Inland, the cuisine is dominated by lamb, rabbit, chicken and the coarse Sicilian sausage, the *salsiccia* (made only of pork mixed with fennel seeds, pepper and a little white wine to taste).

Sicilians always like to round off the meal with a dessert, normally with fruit of the season. On more special occasions, a *dolce* is served, such as a light almond cake often soaked in liqueur. The famous *martorana* – perfectly shaped pieces of fruit made of marzipan – are usually only for decoration.

The Sicilians see themselves as the inventors of ice cream. Even back in the 19th century, the snow on Etna was used as a natural cooling agent and was taken to the towns packed under masses of straw where it was kept in caves and cellars. Sicilian fruit ice cream is always made using fresh fruit. Wild strawberry ice cream is particularly popular. The *granita* is a semi-frozen crystalline dessert made with fruit pulp, almond milk or espresso and is particularly refreshing.

Wine production in Sicily is considerable, both in quantity and quality. Since wine growers have started harvesting grapes earlier, the red and white wines are dry with a good bouquet and – the white wines especially – are light and sparkling. In terms of wine, the island is divided into two: red wines dominate the eastern half, the *Nero d'Avola* grape having been rediscovered more recently. The most important wine-producing areas are in the south east

Always refreshing, always delicious: Sicilians claim to have invented ice cream

and on the northern and eastern flanks of Mount Etna. The western half is definitely a white wine region. The principal regions are the Jato and Belice valleys as well as the plains near Marsala where good dessert wines are also produced.

Apart from wine, the most important drink for the Sicilians is water. Almond milk *(latte di mandorla)* and freshly pressed orange or lemon juice *(spremuta di arancia o di limone)* are also absolutely delicious. And every Sicilian is happy to join friends for a quick *caffè* at a bar at any time.

SHOPPING

Craftwork has a long tradition in Sicily and still dominates many towns and villages. Although many craftsmen have disappeared from the everyday scene, such as tailors, cobblers and basket weavers, Sicily's ceramicists, marionette carvers and rug makers are highly productive. Demand is high not only from tourists – Sicilians themselves have also rediscovered the crafts produced on their island. Good pieces are not always easy to find and have their price – and you'll be unlikely to find a bargain. And then of course there is the mass-produced souvenir trade with all its touristy kitsch.

CERAMICS

Imaginative shapes and bright glazes have always found expression in Sicily's ceramics. Good and top quality pieces can still be found in Caltagirone, Burgio, Sciacca and Santo Stefano di Camastra. The majority of ceramics – with the exception of bright, glazed majolica tiles – are based on traditional pieces. This is especially true of terracotta figures or models of Sicilian carts.

CORAL & JEWELLERY

Trapani was once famous throughout the whole Mediterranean for its coral products. This has virtually disappeared today since the coral reefs off the west coast of Sicily have been entirely decimated and the coral workshops in Torre del Greco near Naples have claimed the coral trade for themselves. Apart from a lot of gaudy merchandise, the *vu cumprà*, hawkers on beaches, also have a few good things, such as jewellery made of silver thread, shells and brightly-coloured pearls.

FASHION & DESIGN

Italian design and fashion can be found in the elegant streets near the Via Etnea in Catania and around the Via Maqueda in Palermo. And of course – although usually much more expensive – in the boutiques in Taormina and on Lipari. The markets are awash with cheap goods and fakes of brand names. In many villages inland, women still embroider and crochet, and weave carpets and blankets by hand.

Majolica, Marsala or marionettes?
When buying souvenirs keep an eye out for quality and hand-crafted Sicilian products

FOOD

Sicily belongs to the underdeveloped south of Italy, large areas of which still exist almost exclusively from farming even today. The chief products are wheat, wine, olive oil, almonds and citrus fruit — way over half of Italy's lemons and oranges are grown in the region. The dominance of agriculture however also has positive aspects: Sicily has now become the leading area in Italy for organic produce. Sicily's wine production is also quite considerable both in quanity and quality. Many wineries have moved away from the traditional, heavy and potent wines of the past to the production of light, aromatic wines. Cheese producers (caseificio) inland and the small sausage manufacturers (salumificio) in the Nebrodi mountains and the high plateau region in the province of Ragusa, will gladly vacuum-pack their cheeses — made from sheep's, cow's or goat's milk — and their meat products.

MARIONETTES

Sicilian marionettes are well known and craftsmen often try to outdo each other in the wonderful expressions they give their figures. But even such puppets are being mass produced now and Charlemagne can be found in all sorts of different variations. Original, second-hand marionettes are to be found at the puppet theatres in Acireale, Monreale and Palermo.

WOVEN BASKETS

Fan palms grow in the far west of the island and their fronds are used to make beautifully shaped baskets, mats and hats to traditional designs. You'll find these in Scopello and San Vito lo Capo.

THE PERFECT ROUTE

FROM THE CITY TO THE SALT WORKS

Start off from the Sicilian capital ① *Palermo* → p. 64 with its wonderful churches, town palaces and lively markets. Then head for ② *Monreale* → p. 71, where one of the greatest Norman cathedrals in the world with its magnificent mosaics should not be missed. The colonnaded temple and Greek amphitheatre in ③ *Segesta* → p. 85 (photo left) rise up spectacularly along a mountain ridge. After passing a number of marble quarries you will reach the mountain town of ④ *Erice* → p. 83, that floats 750m above the plain and the sea. The route takes you past the low lying basins of the salt works before reaching ⑤ *Marsala* → p. 77 where you can sample the local wine in the *bagli*, the wine cellars.

EXPLORING ANCIENT GREEK MARVELS

Take the road to the southeast via Mazara del Vallo to the coast, to ⑥ *Selinunte* → p. 79, one of the most important Greek colonies in Antiquity, now a fascinating archeological site. Keep to the coast heading south east. Before visiting the Greek town of ⑦ *Eraclea Minoa* → p. 81, that lies on a snowy-white promontory, stop off at the beach at the mouth of the Platani for a swim. The next place to head for is ⑧ *Agrigento and the Valle dei Templi* → p. 72 – the largest open-air museum of Greek Antiquity on Sicily. Plan a lot of time for a visit.

HEADING FOR THE GREEN INTERIOR

Turn away from the coast and visit ⑨ *Enna* → p. 49, towering above the surrounding countryside, that itself is dominated by the fortress, Castello Lombardia. ⑩ *Piazza Armerina* → p. 50 is reached after passing through an extensively forested area. 5km (3mi) below, in a verdant river valley, is the *Villa del Casale*, a late Roman imperial villa with magnificent floor mosaics that extend over an incredible 45,000ft². Things move at a gentle pace in the intimate Old Town of ⑪ *Caltagirone* → p. 47 where you can marvel at the brightly coloured tiles on the 130m-long flight of steps and visit ceramicists' studios as well as the ceramics museum.

BAROQUE AND OTHER HIGHLIGHTS

Those interested in architecture can explore a highlight of Sicilian Baroque by visiting the ⑫ *twin towns of Ragusa and Ibla* → p. 53 (photo right), which are also a magnet for gourmets. At Sicily's southern point we head for the sea again. In *Vendicari Nature Reserve* near Noto you will find flamingos and wonderful places to swim. ⑬ *Noto* → p. 51 was rebuilt in the beautiful Baroque style in 1693 after an earth-

Experience the different facets of Sicily – with shorter and longer detours into the heart of the island and around Etna

quake. It wasn't until the 20th-century that the port of ⑭ *Syracuse → p. 55*, with its wonderful medieval and Baroque buildings, reached the size it was in Antiquity. Near Catania, turn off towards ⑮ *Etna → p. 37*. The road climbs to 1880m (6170ft). A cable car or a 4 × 4 will takes you up quite a bit further. Those who want to climb up to the summit and the crater of the volcano (3330m/10,990ft) should take a guide.

ITALY – JUST BEYOND REACH

⑯ *Taormina → p. 43* is the most visited town on Sicily. Going for a stroll or a shopping spree, seeing and being seen – everything happens on the Corso Umberto and the *piazza*. On leaving modern ⑰ *Messina → p. 40*, take the lovely route along the strait as far as *Punta Faro* where Sicily and the Italian mainland are very close. Then head west to ⑱ *Tindari → p. 42* and join pilgrims on a visit to the Black Virgin.

THROUGH THE MOUNTAINS

The road through the ⑲ *Madonie mountains → p. 63* is very twisty so why not stop for a break at one of the *agriturismo* farms? The little town ⑳ *Cefalù → p. 60* lies at the foot of the 270m (885ft) high precipitous limestone *Rocca* which makes the medieval Old Town and the pretty Norman cathedral look tiny in comparison. Leave Cefalù heading west and you will back in Palermo again after 70km (43mi).

1200km (750mi). Driving time: 2 days. Recommended time for this trip: at least 2 weeks. Detailed map of the route on the back cover, in the road atlas and on the pull-out map

THE NORTHEAST

The Peloritani Mountains rise directly behind the narrow coastal strip. The ridge is covered by thick forest in many places, whereas the lower slopes are densely populated garden landscape.

One village runs into the next down the length of the coast. To the north are the seven Aeolian Islands. Etna, Europe's highest active volcano, boasts the whole range of climate zones and vegetation that Sicily has to offer. Despite the catastrophes caused by eruptions, its flanks are densely populated. Breath-taking scenery, art and archeology, beaches, holiday centres such as Acireale and Taormina – everything in the northeast of Sicily is close together.

ACIREALE

(135 E1) *(ɷ K5)* Acireale (pop. 53,000), together with its neighbouring villages, lies on an elevated lava terrace above the Ionian Sea, embedded among countless lemon groves whose green leafy roof is overshadowed by high palm trees.

The Baroque city owes its wealth to the lemon trade and the medicinal springs that have been used since Antiquity. Impressive façades line the main streets and squares. Experience life in the city on one of the three main interconnecting squares and enjoy looking at the municipal hall,

Photo: Taormina, the ancient amphitheatre with a view of Mount Etna

Peaks, gorges, beaches and a lively urban scene – that's Sicily in all its variety. And above all of this towers Mount Etna

the cathedral and the Baroque churches. A pretty street market can be visited in the mornings in the streets behind.

FOOD & DRINK

LA GROTTA
Fish restaurant in a cavern in Santa Maria La Scala. *Closed Tue | Via Scalo Grande | tel. 09 57 64 81 53 | Moderate–Expensive*

BEACHES

The main places to head to for a swim are the fishing villages *Santa Tecla* and *Santa Maria La Scala*.

ENTERTAINMENT

The ● marionette theatre in Acireale has a long tradition. The tourist information office will be able to tell you where and when the next performances are to be held (*Via Oreste Scionti 15 | tel. 0 95 89 19 99 | www.acirealeturismo.it*).

Baroque church in the popular holiday centre Zafferana Etnea

WHERE TO GO

SANT'ALFIO (135 E1) (*Ⓜ K4*)
This mountain village on Mount Etna, 23km (14mi) to the north of Acireale, is well known for its cherries. Sicily's largest tree, the *Centocavalli*, a sweet chestnut estimated to be 1200 years old, can be found on the road to Milo. You can eat well in the restaurant at the organically-run ● 🙂 INSIDER TIP *Azienda Agrituristica Cirasella* nearby (*4 flats | tel. 0 95 96 80 00 | www.cirasellaetna.com | Budget*).

ZAFFERANA ETNEA (135 D1) (*Ⓜ K5*)
21km (13mi) from Acireale, below the awe-inspiring volcanic valley, the Valle del Bove, lies the village Zafferana Etnea, surrounded by gardens and chestnut woods. It is a popular tourist centre due to its healthy climate and good cuisine. INSIDER TIP *Caffè Donna Peppina* on the central Piazza Umberto is well known for its delicious pastries. If you prefer something more substantial try the puff pastry filled with cheese, anchovies or olives. Pleasant, family-run, medium standard hotels include *Primavera dell'Etna* (57 rooms | tel. 09 57 08 23 48 | www.hotel-primavera.it | *Budget–Moderate*), in the middle of an olive grove, and *Airone* (62 rooms | tel. 09 57 08 18 19 | www.hotel-airone.it | *Moderate–Expensive*), above the village on the road to Rifugio Sapienza. Both serve very good plain food. 🙂 *Fermata Spuligni*, a lovingly restored farmhouse with a restaurant, is the perfect place to stay. Its 11 rooms are furnished with 'fair-trade' pieces and textiles (*restaurant closed Mon | Via Matteotti 1 | tel. 09 57 08 20 59 | www.fermataspuligni.com | Budget*).

WHERE TO STAY

Acireale and the little coastal villages around about are particularly focussed on conferences and group tourism. Family-run hotels can be found mostly in the villages slightly higher up Etna.

AGRITURISMO IL LIMONETO 🌿
Located in *Scillichenti* above the cliffs with a garden and view of the sea and Etna. *3 flats | Strada Prov. Acireale–Riposto | tel. 0 95 88 65 68 | www.illimoneto.it | Budget*

B & B AL 22
Right in the centre, furnished in 19th-century style, fridge for guests, WiFi, terrace. *3 rooms | Via San Carlo 22 | tel. 0 95 60 40 88 | www.al22.eu | Budget*

CATANIA

▨▨ **MAP INSIDE BACK COVER**
▨▨ (135 D2) *(ᗰ K5)* **The straight *Via
Etnea* passes through the middle of
Catania (pop. 296,000) from the old
port and across the Cathedral Square
where the other main axis, the *Via
Vittorio Emanuele*, crosses. It ultimately
disappears into the suburbs and merges
into the road to Nicolosi and Mount Etna,
whose main summit is less than 35km
(22mi) from the city.**

The actual craters that have been active in
the past are much closer to Catania, that
itself has been buried under lava several
times. 300 years ago a lava stream filled
in the port that operated at that time, coming to a standstill in front of the *Castello
Ursino*. However, it was the earthquakes
set off by volcanic activity that were much
more destructive. The city owes its homog-
enous Baroque architecture in gloomy
black lava to the last quake in 1693. The
contrasting light-coloured limestone and
rendering has been made just as dark by
industry and cars.

> **CITY WHERE TO START?**
> **Port:** Parking spaces in the
> centre are few and far between so
> it's a good idea to look for one near
> the port (Porto, Via/Piazza Alcala).
> From here, it's just a short walk to
> the central Piazza del Duomo, the
> fish market and Via Etnea. Buses nos.
> 1–4 and 431 N run to the centre from
> the station, the Stazione Centrale,
> from which the narrow gauge Etna
> railway also operates. Long-distance
> coaches depart from the square in
> front of the station and from the
> streets nearby.

▨ **SIGHTSEEING**

CASTELLO URSINO ●
The castle, constructed of black blocks of
lava and with four massive corner towers,
is Catania's only medieval building. In
1669, it became surrounded by streams of
lava. It now houses the *Museo Civico* with
a picture gallery, collections of antiques,
weapons and ceramics, as well as interesting paintings and etchings by local
artists and views of Mount Etna. *Mon–Sat
9am–1pm, Sun 8.30am–1.30pm | Piazza
Federico di Svevia | free entrance*

SANT'AGATA
The Cathedral is dedicated to St Agatha, the
patron saint of Catania, whose reliquary
is housed here. It was built after 1693 on

MARCO POLO HIGHLIGHTS

⭐ **Fish market**
One of Sicily's prettiest markets
is in Catania → p. 36

⭐ **Etna**
The largest active volcano in
Europe → p. 37

⭐ **Ferrovia Circumetnea**
Once round Mount Etna on
the narrow gauge railway
from Catania → p. 39

⭐ **Tindari**
Wonderful view of Lipari & Co
→ p. 42

⭐ **Teatro Greco-Romano**
A view to die for: Mount Etna
and the sea in Taormina → p. 44

⭐ **Alcantara Gorge**
Impressive testimony to the
power of water → p. 45

the site of an earlier Norman church, traces of which can be seen in the transept and apse. A fresco in the sacristy depicts the eruption of Etna in 1669.

PIAZZA DUOMO

Cathedral Square with the black lava elephant is the central hub of the city, with the main shopping streets branching off it. The fish market on Porta Uzeda is just a short walk and the square is surrounded by the huge Baroque town palaces of the nobility and church leaders.

TEATRO BELLINI

The interior of this magnificent building boasts ornate plasterwork, gold, red velvet and huge history paintings. It was inaugurated in 1890 with the Bellini opera 'Norma'.

VIA CROCIFERI

This quiet street of palaces and churches runs parallel to the Via Etnea for part of its length passing villas surrounded by small parks, to the university.

VILLA BELLINI ☙

The park in this district of 19th-century housess is named after the opera composer Vincenzo Bellini. It contains busts of major Sicilian figures as well as an Art Nouveau music pavilion and good views.

FOOD & DRINK

Catania's cooking fuses Sicilian fish dishes with vegetables, cheeses and mushrooms from Mount Etna. The fruit ice cream, that you can find in the Via Etnea in the large pastry shops, is justly famous.

ETOILE D'OR

Chic bar, always full of interesting people. Huge selection from the INSIDER TIP *tavola calda*. *Closed Sun | Via Dusmet 7 | tel. 0 95 32 24 48 | Budget*

INSIDER TIP MAMMUT

Gallery, music bar, restaurant, wine and cocktail bar. *Open from 7.30pm, closed Mon | Via San Lorenzo 20 | tel. 09 57 15 23 55 | www.mammut.ct.it | Budget–Moderate*

OSTERIA ANTICA MARINA

In the heart of the *pescheria* district where the morning market thrives. Seafood in all its varieties. *Closed Wed | Via Pardo 29 | tel. 0 95 34 81 97 | Moderate*

TRATTORIA DEL CAVALIERE

This trattoria in the Old Town offers plain fish dishes and a good buffet. *Closed Wed | Via Paternò 11 | tel. 0 95 31 04 91 | Moderate*

SHOPPING

You should definitely find time for a stroll through Catania's ★ ● *fish market* at the *Porta Uzeda* in the *pescheria* district. It is Sicily's liveliest market which doesn't just sell fish. Don't forget, while you're being distracted by all the colours, smells and sounds, pickpockets like being in the thick of things too.

WHERE TO STAY

AGRITURISMO BAGNARA ☺
(135 D2) (*∅ K5*)

Organic farm with 124 acres of lemon and olive groves, a restaurant and farm shop. 5km (3mi) southwest on the Catania plain. Beach 2km (1¼mi). *13 flats sleeping 2–6 | Contrada Cardinale | tel. 0 95 33 64 07 | www.agribagnara.it | Budget*

SAVONA

Centrally located but quiet, just a few yards from the Piazza Duomo. The plain rooms are large and clean. *30 rooms | Via Emanuele 210 | tel. 0 95 32 69 82 | www.hotelsavona.it | Expensive*

VILLA PARADISO

Art Nouveau villa furnished in the style of the period with a garden and pool, view of the city, private seaside beach. *34 rooms | in San Giovanni della Punta on the Viagrande/Etna road (8km/5mi) | tel. 0957 5124 09 | www.paradisoetna.it | Expensive*

INFORMATION

Bureau del Turismo: Via Vittorio Emanuele 172 | tel. 09 57 42 55 73 | www.comune. catania.it/turismo and *STR: Via Alberto Mario 32 | tel. 09 57 47 74 15*

WHERE TO GO

ETNA ⭐ (135 D1) (𝄞 K4)

Europe's tallest active volcano is 33km (20½mi) from Catania. Mount Etna (3369m/11,050ft) can even be seen from the west coast of Sicily on a clear day. Seen from the side facing inland, it is a yellowy, scorched, bald giant. It only turns a light green in spring when the grass grows. Its snowy cap doesn't always melt completely even in summer.

The best places from which to start exploring Etna's south side are *Nicolosi, Trecastagni* and *Zafferana Etnea*, from which it is only approx. 20km (12½mi) to *Rifugio Sapienza* (1881m/6170ft), where the tarmac road ends and the buses from Catania and Nicolosi stop. *(Depart from Catania/ station square daily 8.15am, Nicolosi 9am, return from Rifugio Sapienza 4.30pm)*. *Rifugio Sapienza* (24 rooms | tel. 0 95 91 53 21 | www.rifugiosapienza.com | Budget) has been extended and turned into a simple hotel. 500m further on is the more comfortable hotel *Corsaro* (20 rooms | tel. 09 59 14 22 | www.hotelcorsaro.it | Moderate). This is where the ● cable car leaves from, the top of which is at an altitude of 2500m (8200ft). Off-road minibuses can take you further up the track as far as *Torre del Filosofo* (2919m/9576ft). A return journey with a guide costs 55 euros. Guides for the summit can be booked at the cable car base station. There is no

Colourful, loud and fascinating: the fish market at Porta Uzeda sells more than just seafood

When Etna erupts, lava up to 1500°C pours down its flanks

way-marked route. Tours on one's own initiative are only allowed as far as Torre del Filosofo and can be dangerous, especially when there is volcanic activity or fog suddenly descends. The temperature of molten lava is between 800–1500°C! (1500–2800° F) Volcanic bombs are projected at supersonic speeds and weigh from 5 kg to more than 1 tonne. Close-up photos are best taken using a telephoto lens. The cordoned off areas are not to prevent you from having a thrilling holiday experience but to keep visitors out of danger.

The eruptions in 2001, 2002/2003 and from January 2011 onwards were the most severe for decades. They not only completely altered the appearance of the summit region. Lava reached right down to densely populated areas and stopped just a few miles short of Nicolosi, Pedara, Zafferana and Milo, having destroyed houses, roads, forests and fields in its wake.

Piano Provenzana and *Rifugio Sapienza* are the principal starting points for tours up to the top of the volcano. Information is available from the *Mountain Guides'*

Office in Nicolosi *(tel. 09 57 97 14 55)* or in Linguaglossa *(tel. 09 57 77 45 02)*, and at the *Etna cable car station (tel. 0 95 91 41 41)*. Up-to-date information about the Etna region can be found online, for example under: *www.ct.ingv.it*, *www.etnaguide.com*, *www.etnaexperience.com* and *www.etna trekking.com*. Winter clothing and hiking boots are essential. And start out early – the summit is often in the clouds later in the day. The hiking season is from mid May until the end of October.

You will pass recent lava fields that smothered woods, fields and gardens on your way to the summit. After just a few years the surface of lava turns from a dark black to a matte grey and the first pioneer plants start to take hold. After 20 years, gorse spreads rapidly. In the early summer the sea of yellow is the most dominant colour on the slopes of the volcano. Forests, mostly of mountain pine and sweet chestnut, prevail. Above 1800m (5900ft), only low-growing shrubs and herbal plants can survive in this volcanic desert.

Nicolosi is the starting point for excursions from the south. Just above it there are waymarked walks to the **INSIDER TIP** *Pineta*

Monti Rossi (the crater created in 1669). Information on the state of roads, the cable car, shelters and guided hikes: *STR (Via Martiri d'Ungheria 36/38 | tel. 0 95 91 15 05 | www.aast-nicolosi.it)*; *SITAS (Piazza Vittorio Emanuele 45 | tel. 0 95 91 41 41 | www.funiviaetna.com)*. Offices of the Etna Park: *Via del Convento 45 | tel. 0 95 82 11 11 | www.parks.it/parco.etna/index.html* and *www.parcoetna.ct.it*

FERROVIA CIRCUMETNEA ⭐

A train ride around Sicily's mighty 'ruler': the narrow gauge railway rattles and shakes its way around lots of bends on its way through this barren landscape on the west flank of Mount Etna. Having reached the highest point, *Maletto* (133 C6) *(㎝ K4)*, it carries on past *Randazzo* (132 C5) *(㎝ K4)* through a black lava desert and lava flows from previous eruptions before dropping down to the coast through a fertile area of gardens, small woods and vineyards.

The journey from *Catania Borgo* to *Randazzo* takes 2 hours; it is another 75 mins from there to *Giarre* (135 E1) *(㎝ K5)*, from where there are connections to Catania and Messina. It is worth skipping a train in Randazzo and taking a walk through the Old Town which is built entirely of black volcanic rock and visiting the Gothic church of *Santa Maria*. Information under *www.circumetnea.it*. Alternatively enjoy this photographic tour: *www.swisseduc.ch/stromboli/etna/virtual-excursions/2005/fce-en.html*

LINGUA-GLOSSA

(133 D6) *(㎝ K4)* This village (pop. 5500) lies amidst luxuriant vineyards and hazelnut groves on a lava flow. As in other villages around Etna, Baroque architecture dominates.

The main church possesses a valuable altar made of cherry wood. This is where the 🥾 panoramic *Mareneve* route begins that links the north side of the volcano with the south.

SIGHTSEEING

There is a small museum on the local natural history and volcanology of Etna in the tourist information building. *Open mornings | free entrance*

SPORTS & ACTIVITIES

Piano Provenzana (132 C6) *(㎝ K4)* at an altitude of 1810m (5938ft) is the most important winter sports arena on Mount Etna and the starting point for 4 × 4 tours towards the summit *(tel. 09 54 03 45 54 | www.etnadiscovery.com)*. This is where the

Up the side of the volcano: hiking up to the crater on Etna's summit

20km (12½mi) *Mareneve* route ('sea and snow') ends. In autumn 2002, this plateau with its hotels, cabins, cable car and forests was buried under molten lava. The congealed black flows are more than impressive. Only the very experienced should attempt a hike to the summit on foot or by mountainbike after having contacted local guides beforehand.

WHERE TO STAY

AGRITURISMO L'ANTICA VIGNA ☺

Organic winery with quiet rooms and good food, direct sales. *10 rooms | on the Randazzo road in Montelaguardia | tel. 0 95 92 40 03 | www.anticavigna.it | Budget*

SHALAI

Restored Baroque palace in the centre, modern design, restaurant. *12 rooms | Via Marconi 25 | tel. 0 95 64 31 28 | www.shalai.it | Moderate–Expensive*

INFORMATION

Pro Loco: Office on the Piazza Annunziata | tel. 0 95 64 30 94 | www.prolocolinguaglossa.it

LOW BUDGET

▶ ♨ *Ostello Odyssey*: youth hostel with rooms with 2 and 4 beds in a modern part of Taormina. *Via Paternò di Biscari 13 | tel. 0 94 22 45 33 u. 34 98 10 77 33 | www.taorminaodyssey.com*

▶ The small, family-run hotel *California* right in the middle of the Old Town in Milazzo has 12 quiet rooms. *Via del Sole 9 | tel. 09 09 22 13 89*

▶ The youth hostel *Ostello Agorà*, in a grand old house in Catania's *pescheria* district, has its own trattoria open 24hrs. *62 beds | Piazza Currò 6 | tel. 09 57 23 30 10 | www.agorahostel.com*

▶ Good, cheap crêpes, both sweet and savoury, are served straight from the pan in *Casa delle Crispelle Cordai* in Acireale. *Evenings only | closed Mon | Via Vittorio Emanuele 3*

MESSINA

(133 E4) *(ﾉﾉ L3)* **For most tourists visiting Sicily, Messina (pop. 243,000) is the gateway to the islands. The city is modern with broad and straight roads.** And its brimming with life – especially in the principle shopping areas *Via San Martino*, the tree-line *Piazza Cairoli* and *Via Garibaldi*. The heart of Messina can be found a little behind these around the *Piazza Duomo* with its magnificent cathedral. But even here as elsewhere in Messina, there are few stones that have been standing longer than 1908 when a terrible earthquake destroyed towns both sides of the straits.

SIGHTSEEING

ACQUARIO (AQUARIUM) ●

Many of the marine creatures – fish, crab, octopuses, mussels, sea anemones – found in the Mediterranean and in the straits can be seen in the 30 basins in the aquarium. *Tue–Sat 9am–1pm, 3pm–7pm, Sun 9am–1pm | Villa Mazzini, Piazza Unità d'Italia | entrance fee 3 euros | www.acquariomessina.it*

CATHEDRAL

The cathedral was originally built in 1197 in the Norman style and rebuilt after the earthquake in 1908 and again after bombing during the war in 1943. The belfry contains an astronomical clock from Strasbourg (1933) that includes a parade of figures at noon.

MUSEO REGIONALE

The museum contains a picture gallery as well as displays of archeological finds, small artefacts and majolica. The most valuable exponents include an altarpiece by the Sicilian Antonello Da Messina and two paintings by Caravaggio. *On the Punta del Faro road | Tue, Thu–Sun 9am–1.30pm, Tue, Thu, Sat also 4pm–7pm | entrance fee 3 euros*

THE FOUNTAIN OF NEPTUNE

On the coastal road in a small park with palm trees and a view over the *Stretto*, next to the *aquarium*.

SANTISSIMA ANNUNZIATA DEI CATALANI

Messina's only building from the Middle Ages. The church was built under the Normans in the 12th and 13th centuries in the Byzantine style, with a dome and extensive ornamental masonry.

Messina Cathedral: simply magnificent from all angles

FOOD & DRINK

AL PADRINO

Lively trattoria in the centre with tasty plain food: lots of vegetables, pasta and fish. *Closed Sun | Via Santa Cecilia 54 | tel. 09 02 92 10 00 | Budget*

INSIDER TIP LE DUE SORELLE

Small restaurant with imaginative Mediterranean cooking and good list of wines. *Closed Mon | Piazza Municipio 4 | tel. 09 04 47 20 | Moderate*

WHERE TO STAY

LE CASE PINTE ❄

B & B at the ferry port (Caronte) with a view of the straits. *3 rooms | Viale della Libertà 251 | tel. 0 90 36 24 09 | www.lecasepinte.com | Budget*

SCILLA E CARIDDI ❄

This modern villa is surrounded by a large garden and furnished in the late 19th-century European style. Good view of the *Stretto*. *8 rooms | Viale Annunziata (3km/2mi to the northeast) | tel. 0 90 35 78 49 | www.scillaecariddi.com | Budget–Moderate*

INFORMATION

STR: Piazza Cairoli 45 | tel. 09 02 93 52 92

MILAZZO

(133 D4) *(ⴑ L3)* **The town (pop. 32,500) is at the beginning of a small peninsula which has several good beaches below the cliffs around Capo Milazzo.**
The partly deserted *Old Town* with its Spanish castle, Baroque cathedral and San Francesco di Paolo monastery, located above the ferry port for crossings to the Aeolian Islands and Naples, is surrounded by a massive circle wall. Information: *AAST / Piazza Duilio 20 | tel. 09 09 22 28 65 | www.aastmilazzo.it*

FOOD & DRINK

SALAMONE A MARE
This elegant restaurant on the scenic road to Capo Milazzo has delicious seafood and courteous service. *Closed Mon | Via Panoramica | tel. 09 09 28 12 33 | Moderate*

WINE BAR AL BAGATTO
Traditional food, good selection of wines, near the harbour in the Old Town. *Only open evenings, closed Wed | Via Regis 11 | tel. 09 09 22 42 12 | Budget*

WHERE TO STAY

PETIT HOTEL ☼ ☺
Restored to exacting environmental standards, restaurant with organic food and 'Libera Terra' products. *9 rooms | Via dei Mille 37 | tel. 09 09 28 67 84 | www.petit hotel.it | Moderate–Expensive*

WHERE TO GO

SAN FRATELLO AND THE NEBRODI MOUNTAINS (132 B5) *(ⴑ J3–4)*
In Sant'Agata di Militello, the road over the pass forks off to *Cesarò* and leads into the heart of the *Nebrodi Park (www.parco deinebrodi.it)* some 100km (62mi) further on. Its 1800m (5900ft) high mountain range is covered in extensive grazing land and thick beech woods. *San Fratello* is a typical mountain village well known for horse breeding. Hikers can find board and lodging on the pass in the INSIDER TIP *Villa Miraglia (5 rooms | tel. 0 95 69 73 97 | www.villamiraglia.it | Budget–Moderate)*.

TINDARI ★ ☼ (132 C4) *(ⴑ K3)*
The cliff of Tindari, 30km (18½mi) west of Milazzo, is a landmark on the north coast that cannot be missed. Below the 260m (850ft) high cliff face of the promontory, a sandbank enclosing a seawater lagoon and lakes stretches into the bay. The Black Madonna in the pilgrim church attracts the faithful from all of Sicily. The sandbank and the Aeolian Islands can be seen from the square in front of the church. The plateau is the site of the *ancient Greek city of Tyndaris (daily 9am–7pm | entrance fee 4 euros)* with an amphitheatre and basilica.

The organic 😊 *Agriturismo Santa Margherita* estate *(18 rooms, 2 flats | tel. O 94 13 97 03 | www.agriturismosantamargherita. com | Budget–Moderate)* has a garden overlooking the sea, a restaurant, riding stables and mountainbikes for hire.

TAORMINA

⊠ MAP INSIDE BACK COVER

(133 D6) (𝄢 L4) ⚶ **The best-known and most-visited holiday destination on Sicily (pop. 11,000) is situated on a prominent hill at the end of the Peloritani mountain ridge high above the sea with an unforgettable view of Etna.** The town centre is surrounded by villas and hotels dating from the 19th and 20th centuries. The picture of an enchanting medieval town unfurls to either side of the main shop-lined street, the *Corso Umberto*, between the town gates *Porta Messina* and *Porta Catania*, with castellated

palaces, alleyways and small squares all linked by steps. The outskirts of Taormina suffer from the traffic; the centre is however an oasis. The *Piazza IX Aprile* half-way down the Corso, with its gate into the heart of the Old Town is a meeting place at all times of day, and the famous *Caffè Wunderbar* with the best view of Etna and the coast.

SIGHTSEEING

CATHEDRAL

The cathedral with its castellated façade dates from Norman times. The interior is plain. The *Baroque fountain with the Centaur*, Taormina's emblem, graces the square outside.

PALAZZO CORVAIA

The *palazzo* is one of the elegant palaces of the nobility dating from Norman times. The interior, which is open to the public, also houses the tourist information office.

The view from the Teatro Greco-Romano over Taormina and the coastline extends for miles

TEATRO GRECO-ROMANO ★ ☼
The most impressive view of the coastline and the huge volcano can be enjoyed from the semicircle of this amphitheatre. It was hewn out of the natural stone and, in summer, provides a setting for classical theatrical and musical performances. *Daily 9am–7pm | entrance fee 8 euros*

FOOD & DRINK

INSIDER TIP CASA GRUGNO
Culinary fantasies in a Gothic palace. Garden terrace. Closed Sun evenings and Mon | *Via Santa Maria dei Greci | tel. 0 94 22 12 08 | www.casagrugno.it | Expensive*

NINO
Superb seafood from *antipasti* to the main course prepared with the day's fresh catch. *Closed Tue | on Letoianni beach (7km/4½mi to the north) | Via Rizzo 29 | tel. 0 94 23 61 47 | Moderate*

PORTA MESSINA
Good cheap pizzas, pasta, mussels and fish can be found at the Old Town gate. *Closed Wed | Largo Giove Serapide | tel. 0 94 22 32 05 | Budget–Moderate*

BEACHES

The *Isola Bella* and *Mazzarò* beaches have large pebbles and are very crowded. There's more room in *Letoianni* to the north, and *Capo Schisò* and *San Marco* to the south. The quickest way to get to Mazzarò is by cable car. Buses to the beaches run frequently between Capo Schisò and Letoianni.

ENTERTAINMENT

The *Corso Umberto* and the *piazza* next to the clocktower are the liveliest places. Discos are generally on the outskirts.

CAFFÈ WUNDERBAR
The bar of bars, equally suitable for the less famous for seeing and being seen. *Piazza IX Aprile (Corso)*

WHERE TO STAY

GRAND HOTEL TIMEO & VILLA FLORA
This elegant villa set in lovely gardens is the top address not only in Taormina but in Sicily as a whole. *85 rooms | Via Teatro Greco 59 | tel. 0 94 22 38 01 | www.grandhoteltimeo.com | Expensive*

ISABELLA
Some rooms have sea views. *32 rooms | Corso Umberto 58 | tel. 0 94 22 31 53 | www.gaishotels.com | Moderate*

INSIDER TIP IL PICCOLO GIARDINO – KÉPOS
Hotel and restaurant with 25 rooms, roof garden, pool. Unusual dishes fusing seafood and vegetables as well as Sicilian classics such as *pasta alla Norma*. *Salita Lucio Denti 4 | tel. 0 94 22 34 63 | www.ilpiccologiardino.it | depending on room and season Budget–Expensive| restaurant Moderate, for hotel guests Budget*

LA IGIEA
Art Nouveau villa above the Old Town, 12 plain, attractive rooms. *Via Circonvallazione 28 | tel. 09 42 62 52 75 | www.villaigiea.com | Budget–Moderate*

VILLA SCHULER
Villa with garden and a lovely view of the coast. *26 rooms | Piazzetta Bastione 16 | tel. 0 94 22 34 81 | www.hotelvillaschuler.com | Moderate–Expensive*

INFORMATION

STR: Palazzo Corvaja | tel. 0 94 22 32 43 | www.gate2taormina.com

WHERE TO GO

ALCANTARA GORGE ★
(133 D5) *(M K4)*

18km (11mi) west of Taormina the River Alcantara and its waterfalls have cut a narrow gorge through the basalt up to 50m (165ft) deep. Can be accessed down steps from the road to *Francavilla* as well as by a lift *(www.parcoalcantara.it)*. Paddle in the cold water or hire wellies at the entrance! You can enjoy plain country cooking in *Paradise (closed Mon | Viale Jannuzzo 2 | tel. 0 94 24 74 00 | Budget)* on the road above the gorge, which also has tables outside.

CASTELMOLA
(133 D5) *(M L4)*

This tiny mountain eyrie with its much lauded views (ruins of the *castello*) is 5km (3mi) away, almost vertically above Taormina. Slightly further down is the hotel *Villa Sonia (44 rooms | tel. 0 94 22 80 82 | www.hotelvillasonia.com | Moderate–Expensive)*.

GIARDINI NAXOS (133 D6) *(M L4)*

This tourist resort famous for its beaches is 6km (3¾mi) south of Taormina, wedged in between main roads and the railway line. The shore area is however particularly attractive near the excavation site of *Ancient Naxos*, the oldest Greek city on Sicily with impressive megalithic stone walls. The stylish hotel *Arathena Rocks (49 rooms | tel. 0 94 25 13 49 | www.hotelarathena.it | Moderate)* is right on the sea in a private park. Information: *Lungomare Tysandros 54 | tel. 0 94 25 10 10 | www.strgiardini.it*

SAVOCA (133 D–E5) *(M L4)*

Mummified corpses can be seen in the *Chiesa dei Cappuccini* in this mountain village 24km (15mi) to the north in the Peloritani Mountains on the road from Santa di Riva to Casalvecchio Siculo. The Norman and Byzantine church INSIDER TIP *Pietro e Paolo*, which boasts Arabian intarsia work and a steep-sided dome, is situated below Sant'Alessio Siculo near Scifi in the *Fiumara d'Agrò* valley in a lemon grove.

The remnants of a fishing idyll on the beach in Giardini Naxos with Taormina above

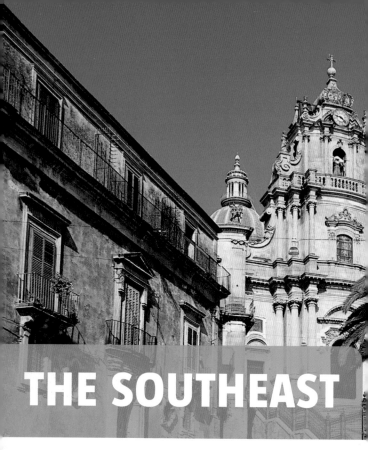

THE SOUTHEAST

Sicilians often talk about the 'island on the island'. Rising behind the flat coastal plains with their dense plantations of almond trees, olive groves and citrus fruit, is the karst landscape of gorges and rivers of the Hyblaean Mountains (Monti Iblei), which rise to a height of almost 1000m (3280ft).

The lush fertile plains are in stark contrast to the more than sparse vegetation in the mountains where treeless grazing land, divided by miles of stone walls and with a scattering of isolated farms, stretches as far as the horizon. Trees grow in profusion in the valleys following the course of the streams and rivers, and gorges boast dense jungles of oleander, Spanish cane as tall as houses, violet blossoming Monk's Pepper and brambles. The upper flanks of the gorges that can be easily reached from the plains above, were the first places to be settled. In 2011, the large limestone plateau with its deep ravines became Sicily's first national park – one of the largest in Italy.

Ispica, Modica and the twin towns of Ragusa and Ibla have spectacular locations, as does the isolated necropolis of Pantalica. All of them have been built in the light-coloured limestone of the area which is easy to work when first quarried before becoming harder after contact with

Photo: San Giorgio in Ragusa

Contrasting Sicilian highlights: fertile plains, barren mountains, ancient cities and Baroque towns

the air and taking on a grey or dark yellow patina. No other stone enabled sculptors to live out their fantasies so easily. Portals with faces and ornamental scrolling, sills and balconies, façades with mythical creatures, gnomes, nymphs, monsters, squiggles and pillars are characteristic features of these towns. This is especially true of those built after the devastating earthquake of 1693.

CALTAGIRONE

(134 B3) *(ⓜ H–J6)* ★ This town (pop. 39,000) with its church towers and domes can be seen from a long way away on a mountain peak.

The streets are narrow and, apart from the famous *majolica staircase*, there are many other plain flights of steps. The grand stair-

142 steps with brightly-coloured majolica tiles lead up to Santa Maria al Monte

case of 1608, with its decorative ceramic tiles of a more recent date, connects the lower town with the *Palazzo della Corte Capitaniale* and the main square with the principle church, *Santa Maria al Monte*, in the upper town. In the *Villa Comunale* next to the ceramics museum, is the *Teatrino*, a pavilion with majolica tiles.

SIGHTSEEING

MUSEO REGIONALE DELLA CERAMICA ●
Ceramics from Antiquity to the present day and Sicilian majolica from the Renaissance and Baroque periods. *Daily 9am–6.30pm | Giardino Pubblico | entrance fee 4 euros*

FOOD & DRINK

CORIA
Two small dining rooms near the Staircase and two chefs who like experimenting and who love fresh herbs and seafood. Try the couscous with fish sauce instead of the usual pasta or sweet-and-sour stuffed rabbit and orange salad. *Closed Sun even-*

ing and Mon | *Via Infermeria 24 | tel. 09 33 33 46 15 | Moderate*

POMARA
Rustic restaurant in neighbouring *San Michele di Ganzaria*, aromatic country cooking with big portions. Hotel *(40 rooms). Tel. 09 33 97 69 76 | www.hotel pomara.com | Moderate*

SHOPPING

CERAMICS
Many quality pieces are still made traditionally in the ceramic workshops in Caltagirone, where the decoration and glazing of expensive items is carried out with meticulous precision. If you like, you can also watch the craftsmen at work in their studio in the Old Town. Works are exhibited in the courtyard of the *Palazzo Corte Capitaniale* and in the shops in the *Galleria Don Sturzo*.

WHERE TO STAY

IL PICCOLO ATTICO
B & B in the middle of the Old Town not far from the Staircase, lovely 🌿 roof terrace

with a view over the town. *3 rooms, 1 flat | Via Infermeria 82 | tel. 0 93 32 15 88 | Budget*

INFORMATION

Azienda di Turismo in the *Palazzo Libertini*: tel. 0 93 35 38 09 | www.comune.calta girone.ct.it

ENNA

(134 A2) (*⌘ H5*) ☀ **The provincial capital Enna (pop. 28,000), perched more than 900m above sea level, is called the 'belvedere' (panoramic viewpoint) of Sicily due to its far-reaching views over central Sicily and to the mountain village Calascibetta opposite, Mount Etna and the mountains to the north.**

The fortifications dating from Norman era and the Hohenstaufen dynasty, such as the *Castello di Lombardia* and the *Torre Pisana* at the highest point of the town, as well as the octagonal tower, the *Torre di Federico II*, allegedly designed by Emperor Frederick II, are well worth seeing.

FOOD & DRINK

LA BRACE
Family-run trattoria on the road from Enna to the mountain eyrie Calascibetta. Wide selection of dishes. *Closed Mon | tel. 0 93 53 46 99 | Budget*

CENTRALE
Good country fare is served in this family-run restaurant. *Closed Sat | Piazza VI Dicembre 9 | tel. 09 35 50 09 63 | Budget*

WHERE TO STAY

LA CASA DEL POETA ☺
B & B in a restored 19th-century country house located above Lago Pergusa, with pool, surrounded by cypress and olive trees. Modern interior, rooms decorated with literary texts and graphic works; writing and reading room. Organic breakfast. *26 rooms | tel. 32 96 27 49 18 | www.lacasadel poeta.it | Moderate*

RIVIERA
On Lago Pergusa with a garden, view of the lake, pool, good inexpensive food (*Budget*). *26 rooms | tel. 09 35 54 12 67 | www.rivierahtl.it | Moderate*

MARCO POLO HIGHLIGHTS

★ **Caltagirone**
Flights of steps, palaces and churches are decorated with majolica tiles → p. 47

★ **Piazza Armerina**
Mosaics cover a vast area in the Roman Villa del Casale → p. 50

★ **Noto**
This small Baroque town was planned on a grid system → p. 51

★ **Museo Regionale Archeologico**
A tour through the 15,000-year history of Syracuse → p. 57

★ **Ortygia**
Nowhere else are so many testimonies to Antiquity, the Middle Ages and the Baroque to be found at such close quarters as in the Old Town in Syracuse → p. 57

★ **Pantalica**
More than 5000 tombs hewn into the rock → p. 59

STR: Piazza Napoleone Colajanni 6 | tel. 09 35 50 08 75 | www.ennaturismo.info (with excellent material on the region)

WHERE TO GO

MORGANTINA ☂ **(134 B2)** *(∅ H6)*
The ancient city is 42km (26mi) southeast of Enna on a mountain ridge with views extending to Etna and the sea. The wind and the silence dominate the 2000-year-old paved streets, the well-preserved amphitheatre and the huge terraced *agorà* *(daily 8am–sunset | entrance fee 4 euros)*. INSIDER TIP Statues of gods from illicit excavations, previously at the Getty Museum in Los Angeles and since returned to Italy, are on show in *Aidone* in the *Museo Archeologico (Tue–Sun 8am–6.30pm | 4 euros)*.

PIAZZA ARMERINA ★ **(134 A3)** *(∅ H6)*
This town with its colourful and silver church domes lies on a mountain ridge

surrounded by eucalyptus groves, hazel woods and orchards, 34km (21mi) southeast of Enna. 5km (3mi) down a valley, a turning leads to the excavation site of the ● *Villa Romana del Casale (following completion of restoration, projected opening times: daily 8.30am–6.30pm, in winter until 4pm | entrance fee approx. 10 euros | www.villaromanadelcasale.it)*. The floor mosaics from Antiquity of this Unesco World Heritage Site are among the most extensive and beautiful to have survived. The techniques used and the motifs would suggest artists from North Africa. The villa was probably the country seat and hunting lodge of a Roman emperor from the 4th century. The ground plan of the site, under protective Plexiglass structures, is clearly recognisable. It includes public and private quarters, the thermal baths, halls, bed-chambers, privy, kitchen, servants' rooms and, at the centre, the peristyle, the internal garden surrounded by a colonnade. Raised walkways lead to the 'Chamber of the Ten Maidens' with its famous mosaic of girls performing sports dressed in bikini-like garments.

The 😊 *Agriturismo Bannata* farmhouse is on the edge of a wood 6km (3¾mi) north of Piazza. Contemporary art exhibitions and music events are held in the rooms with natural stone and terracotta floors, modern furniture and antiques. Light food made to old recipes is served in the restaurant. Bread, biscuits, vegetables and wine come from their own organic production. *(SS 117 as far as km 41 | tel. 09 35 68 13 55 | www.agriturismobannata. it | Moderate, restaurant for house guests Budget)*. Il Fogher (closed Mon | tel. 09 35 68 41 23 | Moderate), which serves excellent and imaginative Sicilian food, is located on the road to Enna after the turn to Morgantina (2km/1¼mi). Information: *STR | Via Generale Muscarà | in the village, not at the villa! | tel. 09 35 68 02 01*

SICILIA FASHION VILLAGE
(134 B2) *(ᗰ J5)*

30km (18½mi) east of Enna, right next to the motorway, is Sicily's largest outlet centre with 120 clothes shops, bars and restaurants, all built to look like a small 18th-century Sicilian town. *(Mon–Fri 10am–8pm, Sat/Sun 10am–9pm | A 19 Catania–Palermo, exit Dittaino | www.siciliafashionvillage.it).* In *Raddusa*, 15km (9mi) further south, ● ☺ *Casa-Museo del Tè* traces the history of tea with 600 different sorts and 500 teapots from all over the world. You can take part in a tea ceremony in the *salon* or enjoy the Asian-style food. And you'll be doing a good deed too: the company sponsors school and health projects in the third world. *Daily 9am–1pm, 5pm–midnight | Via Garibaldi 45 | advance booking necessary, tel. 09566 2193 | www.lacasadelte.it | free entrance | Budget*

NOTO

(135 D5) *(ᗰ K7)* ★ **This Baroque town (pop. 24,000) is a Unesco World Heritage Site located at the foot of the Hyblaean Mountains above the coastal plain with its dense olive groves that are as shady as a wood.**

The medieval *Noto Antica* fell victim to the earthquake of 1693. The ruins can be seen 9km (9½mi) further inland.

Pure Baroque: the balcony supports at the Palazzo Villadorato in Noto

SIGHTSEEING

THE TOWN OF PALACES

The principle churches, palaces, squares and flights of steps can be found in the elegant district of Noto along the three parallel main thoroughfares. The central one, the *Corso Vittorio Emanuele*, finishes at the representative town gates. It covers a large area including parks and squares and is lined by town palaces, opening up half-way down to the *Piazza Duomo* with a broad view of steps and façades. This is where the spiritual and worldy centres of power stand face to face – the *cathedral* and the *Palazzo Ducezio*.

FOOD & DRINK

TRATTORIA DEL CROCIFISSO

Family-run country-style restaurant that attracts both locals and tourists alike. *Closed Wed | Via Principe Umberto 46 | tel. 09 31 57 11 51 | Budget*

NOTO

BEACHES & SPORTS

Swimming and bird-watching are two options on the fine sandy beach in *Marina di Noto*, hiking and swimming in the *Vendicari* nature reserve, and swimming in the *Cava Grande* (Noto–Palazzolo road).

WHERE TO STAY

TERRA DI SOLIMANO 🖤
(135 D5) (*ſ⊞ K7*)
This organically-run historical manor on the road to Noto Antica offers bed and breakfast. *8 rooms | tel. 09 31 83 66 06 | www. terradisolimano.it | Budget*

VILLA CANISELLO
Former farmhouse with a large garden. *6 rooms | Via Pavese 1 | tel. 09 31 83 57 93 | www.villacanisello.it | Budget*

WHERE TO GO

CAVA D'ISPICA (134 C5) (*ſ⊞ J–K8*)
The 12km (7½mi) long karst gorge ends just below the Baroque town of *Ispica*, 27km (17mi) southwest of Noto. The main access to the gorge, which boasts Byzantine rock churches and subterranean catacombs *(daily 8am–5pm)* is on the road from Rosolini to Modica. The *Parco della Forza (daily 8am–5pm)* in Ispica, with its cave churches and wall fragments, takes you an easy 3km (1¾mi) into the gorge. Good food can be had at the *Locanda del Borgo* in the neighbouring village of Rosolini *(closed Mon | Via Controscieri 11 | tel. 09 31 85 05 14 | Moderate)*.

NOTO ANTICA & PALAZZOLO ACREIDE
While on this 96km (60mi) tour, take the road in Noto to the *Convento della Scala*, one of the most isolated Baroque pilgrim churches. Just a little further on, park the car on the approach road to *Noto Antica* (135 D5) (*ſ⊞ K7*). The massive gateway and walls are the most impressive remains of this town destroyed in 1693, located on a high-lying plain. Here and there traces of walls can be seen above the weeds, including columns and church portals on the near end of the plateau. Returning to the main road, the 287, you can make a 6km

Cava Grande: the little River Cassíbile carved out these wonderful 'bathtubs'

(3¾mi) detour along the by-road to Avola to INSIDER TIP *Cava Grande*, a broad gorge approached down steps carved out of the cliff face from the car park. Good shoes are needed to climb down into the gorge 200m below, as the steps can be slippery. Once there, wide paths lead to the crystal-clear river with waterfalls, lakes and sandbanks. *Palazzolo Acreide (135 D4) (Ø K7)* dominates a hill, the highest point of which was the site occupied by the ancient town Akrai. Baroque craftsmen have also created an abundance of decorative elements, including faces and mythological figures, out of soft yellow limestone and wrought iron. The façades around the huge piazza are especially richly decorated. From here, a passage leads to the side streets and to the folk museum, *Casa Museo Antonino Uccello (daily 9am–1pm and 2.30pm–7pm | entrance fee 2 euros)*. Good food is served in *Trattoria Andrea (closed Tue | Via Maddalena 24 | tel. 09 31 88 14 88 | Budget)*. Far-reaching views can be enjoyed over the southeast of Sicily from the ancient ✺ *Acropolis (daily 9am–shortly before sunset | entrance fee 4 euros)* which has a small amphitheatre.

PORTO PALO DI CAPO PASSERO (135 E6) (Ø K8)

This small town, 28km (17½mi) from Noto on Sicily's southern-most point, with its busy fishing port, has become a popular holiday destination thanks to the extensive dunes and beaches to the north near *Vendicari* and the sandy bays. Surfers come for the strong winds. Plain accommodation and good food is available in the modern holiday hotels *Jonic (12 rooms | tel. 09 31 84 27 23 | Budget)* and *Vittorio (25 rooms | tel. 09 31 84 21 81 | Budget–Moderate)*. The restaurant *Cialoma (Piazza Regina Margherita | tel. 09 31 84 17 72 | Moderate)* in *Marzamemi*, the neighbouring fishing village that consists of a few flat-roofed stone huts, serves everything the sea with its rich fishing grounds has to offer.

INSIDER TIP VENDICARI & VILLA ROMANA TELLARO (135 D6) (Ø K8)

Vendicari Nature Reserve incorporates wide sandy beaches, dunes with Mediterranean *macchia*, swamps and lagoons, which are a unique paradise for birds, is 8km (5mi) long and up to 1000m wide. 250 different breeds of bird live here, including flamingos, storks, herons, ibis and spoonbills *(www.oasivendicari.net)*.

The *Villa Romana di Tellaro* is on the Porto Palo road right next to the sea, at the north boundary of Vendicari Nature Reserve. Late Roman mosaics of hunting scenes and heroic figures from the *Iliad* can now be viewed after 30 years of excavation *(daily 9am–7pm | entrance fee 6 euros | www.villaromanadeltellaro.com)*.

RAGUSA

(134 C5) (Ø J7) **Ragusa (pop. 73,000) is the capital of the smallest and wealthiest province on Sicily. The oil fields, that have now been fully exhausted, launched a short industrial boom around 1960.**

The novels in the 'Commissario Montalbano' series were filmed for television in the little towns and coastal villages in this province. His house is in Puntasecca; Donnalucata is the port of the fictional town 'Vigata'. The Baroque setting of Ragusa Ibla, Scicli and Modica turned the series into a visual delight. A list of places where the series was filmed can be found under *www.giovannisarto.it*.

Ragusa has two centres: the more modern *Ragusa* with its wide streets, and the small Baroque *Ibla* of the nobility, clerics, craftspeople and agricultural workers, with its flights of steps, narrow alleyways and little squares.

SIGHTSEEING

SAN GIORGIO
The main church in Ibla, with its imposing façade and flight of steps, is an exceptional example of the Baroque style in Sicily.

SAN GIORGIO VECCHIO ✳
The ruins of a Norman church with a lovely portal. From the park behind you have a fantastic view of the town above and the gorge.

FOOD & DRINK

CUCINA E VINO
Family-run trattoria in the Old Town of Ibla serving pasta, lamb and fish. *Closed Wed | Via Orfanotrofio 91 | tel. 09 32 68 64 47 | Budget*

DUOMO
In the Old Town of Ibla, exquisite cuisine prepared with considerable expertise and the best ingredients. *Closed Sun | Via Boccheri 31 | tel. 09 32 65 12 65 | www. ristoranteduomo.it | Expensive*

MAJORE
This restaurant lies in the centre of the neighbouring village Chiaramonte Gulfi. Popular among meat-lovers especially those with a hankering for hearty pork dishes. *Closed Mon and in July | Via Martiri Ungheresi | tel. 09 32 92 80 19 | www. majore.it | Budget*

WHERE TO STAY

AGRITURISMO VILLA ZOTTOPERA ☺
17th-century manorial farm, excellent food, cookery courses, organic production of olive oil, wine and vegetables. *5 flats | 8km (5mi) towards Chiaramonte | tel. 09 32 24 40 18 | www.villazottopera.it | Moderate*

MONTREAL
Well-presented, centrally located town hotel. *50 rooms | Via San Giuseppe 8 | tel. 09 32 62 11 33 | www.montrealhotel.it | Moderate*

INFORMATION

STR: Via Giordano Bruno 3 | tel. 09 32 67 58 37 | www.comune.ragusa.gov.it/turismo

WHERE TO GO

DONNAFUGATA (134 B5) *(𝄢 J7)*
This palace and its extensive park is 15km (9mi) from Ragusa. In the 19th century towers and battlements were added and the interior decked out with chandeliers, mirrors, frescos and antique furniture *(Tue, Thu, Sun 9am–1pm, 2.45pm–4.30pm, Wed, Fri, Sat 9am–1pm | entrance fee incl. park 6 euros)*. Luchino Visconti filmed 'The Leopard' here. The *Trattoria Al Castello* which serves simple dishes is housed in the former stables *(closed Mon | tel. 09 32 61 92 60 | Budget)*.

MODICA (134 C5) *(𝄢 J7)*
The former capital of the county of Modica, identical to the present-day province of Ragusa, is 15km (9mi) south at the base of two karst gorges that meet at the central square. The Old Town, with its narrow alleyways and flights of steps, climbs the steep slopes, whereas the two main streets with their promenades run along the valley which is wide enough to accommodate churches and the palaces of the nobility. The dominant architectural style here is also Baroque, fine examples of which are the main church, *San Pietro* in the lower town, and *San Giorgio* with five portals and an impressive flight of 250 steps. *Hotel Bristol (18 rooms | Via Risorgimento 8 b | tel. 09 32 76 28 90 | www.hotelbristol. it | Moderate)* is in the upper town. If you

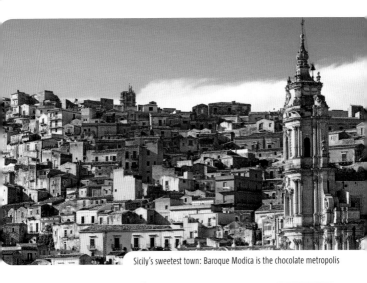

Sicily's sweetest town: Baroque Modica is the chocolate metropolis

choose *Monoresort* you can stay in one of the restored houses in the Old Town with modern designer interiors *(4 flats | tel. 09 32 45 33 08 | www.monoresort.com | Expensive)*. In the elegant *Fattoria delle Torri* in the middle of the Old Town, you can eat like in the olden days *(closed Mon | Vivo Napolitano 14 | tel. 09 32 75 12 86 | Moderate)*.

Modica is considered the Sicilian centre of the chocolate industry. The *Corso Umberto* is perfect for a 'chocolate tour': for example in *Antica Dolceria Bonajuto*, the *Laboratorio Dolciario Don Giuseppe Puglisi* or in ☺ *Quetzal* and ☺ *La Bottega Solidale*, in which only fairtrade products are processed. *Information: Ufficio Turismo | Corso Umberto 141 | tel. 09 32 75 92 04*

The neighbouring Baroque town *Scicli* (pop. 26,000), which is only a few roads wide, winds its way down a gorge. You can get a good impression of its unusual location from the church of San Matteo, situated further up. Art historians consider the *Palazzo Beneventano* to be the most beautiful Baroque building on the island.

WHERE TO START?
Ortygia: Syracuse's station is on the outskirts of the city but a good bus service operates to the Old Town of Ortygia on the island. Buses 1 and 2 connect the Old Town with the excavation sites, bus 3 with the museum, both in the modern city on the mainland. There are carparks on the island at Foro Vittorio Emanuele and on Piazza Marina (harbour), as well as at the excavation sites (Viale Teocrito, Corso Gelone, Viale Augusto).

SYRACUSE

MAP ON P. 56
(135 E4) (*ℳ L7*) The town Siracusa with a population of 124,000, is situated on a limestone plateau that drops down to the sea, and on the island of Ortigia, that has been linked to the mainland by a bridge for 2500 years.

SYRACUSE

The modern part of the city on the mainland accounts for only a small part of the footprint once occupied by ancient Syrakusai. The huge elevated site of Epipolai, west of the modern city, which stretches as far as Castel Eurialo and is no longer inhabited today, was – 2000 years ago – the largest district in the ancient city which had a population of half a million. The flat rocky island did not just offer protection and an excellent harbour: the freshwater source, created by the nymph Arethusa in mythology, attracted settlers from an early date.

Syrakusai was the economical and political as well as the scientific and cultural centre of Sicily in Antiquity. At times it was the largest city in all of Hellas. Plundered by the Romans, it lost much of its glamour. During the Early Christian era, Syracuse had

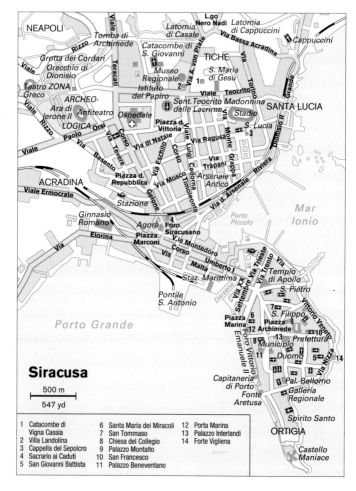

Siracusa

500 m
547 yd

Ortygia: the cafés on the promenade – each with a sea view

a large Christian community and meetings were held in the catacombs where the Apostle Paul also preached. In the Byzantine period it was the capital of Sicily, only losing its significance under Arab and Norman rule.

SIGHTSEEING

GALLERIA REGIONALE IN THE PALAZZO BELLOMO

Important paintings and sculptures by Sicilian artists can be seen in this beautifully restored medieval palace in Ortygia, as well as ceramics, carpets and artistic artefacts. *Tue–Sat 9am–7pm, Sun 9am–1pm | Via Capodieci 16 | entrance fee 6 euros*

SAN GIOVÀNNI CATACOMBS

The extensive Early Christian catacombs can be accessed through San Giovanni church in modern Syracuse. *Daily 9am–12.30pm and 2.30pm–5.30pm | entrance fee 5 euros*

MUSEO REGIONALE ARCHEOLOGICO ★

Sicily's largest museum contains prehistoric artefacts as well as finds from Ancient Greek and Roman sites throughout Sicily. The finds from Syracuse alone could easily fill several museums. Highlights include the *Venus Landolina* and an archaic *kouros* – a statue of a male youth – made of limestone. *Tue–Sat 9am–6pm, Sun 9am–1pm | Viale Teocrito | entrance fee 8 euros*

ORTYGIA ★

The main bridge leads to *Piazza Pancali*, where the gigantic dressed stones and columns of the *Temple of Apollo* (6th century BC) cannot be missed. In the morning, the square and the roads nearby leading to *Porto Piccolo* – the fishing port – is a sea of market stalls and people. *Corso Matteotti* leads to *Piazza Archimede*, into the heart of the Old Town. The majority of the palaces of the noble families and leading figures of the church line the square and the promenade *Via Maestranza* that leads off it. In several of the smaller streets, especially those leading to the sea, many houses stand empty.

The long and narrow *Piazza Duomo* is dominated by the cathedral's Baroque façade that is subdivided by columns. The surprising and completely preserved *Temple of Athena* from the 5th century BC lies behind it. The *Fountain of Arethusa* below the promenade along the shore gushes into a fishpond planted with papyrus. *Castello Maniace*, the medieval fortress, is part of the former defensive wall and offers wonderful views down the coast *(Tue–Sat 9.30am–1.30pm | entrance fee 4 euros)*.

PARCO ARCHEOLOGICO DELLA NEAPOLI

The archeological area on the outskirts of the new town covers just a small part of ancient Syracuse and several *latomie* – quarries from Antiquity. A shady path from the entrance leads to the right to the *Roman amphitheatre*, that is largely hewn directly out of the rock face. Large public sacrifices were celebrated on the *Altar of Hieron* (198m long, 23m wide, 3rd century BC). The *Greek theatre*, with tiers also cut out of the rock, could seat more than 15,000 spectators. It is now used for classical performances. *Latomia del Paradiso* is the largest quarry in the ancient urban settlement and now a cool and shady park. The *Orecchio di Dionisio* ('Ear of Dionysius') is an artificial cave – a subterranean quarry – 65m long and 23m high, which was reputedly used as a prison. The unusual acoustics that make even whispers clearly audible, was perfect for listening to suspects. *Daily 9am–sunset | entrance fee 10 euros*

SANTUARIO DELLA MADONNINA DELLE LACRIME

The plaster statue of the Virgin Mary, which has cried tears and performed miracles since 1953, is kept in a building with a diameter of 90m and a 76m-high conical roof that dominates the city. The church

Tragedies have been performed in this Greek theatre since 470 BC

Santa Lucia del Sepolcro, which boasts Caravaggio's major work *The Burial of Saint Lucy*, is also in the new district of the city.

FOOD & DRINK

DON CAMILLO
A wide selection of delicious seafood dishes prepared to traditional recipes. On the main road from Ortygia. *Closed Sun | Via Maestranza 96 | tel. 0 93 16 71 33 | Moderate*

VITE E VITELLO
Plain dishes of pork, veal, fresh pasta and sweetbreads can be found in this former osteria. *Closed Sun | Piazza Corpaci 1 | tel. 09 31 46 42 69 | Budget*

BEACHES & SPORTS

Good sandy beaches can be found in *Fontane Bianche* (135 E5) *(∅ L7)*. Walkers will enjoy a hike through the *Anapo Valley* and in *Pantalica* (135 D4) *(∅ K7)*.

WHERE TO STAY

DOMUS MARIAE
Luxuriously revamped monastery building with 16 rooms. *Via Vittorio Veneto 76 | Ortigia | tel. 0 93 12 48 54 | www.sistemia. it/domusmariae | Expensive*

GIUGGIULENA
B & B above the cliffs (Neapolis). *9 rooms | Via Pitagora da Reggio 35 | tel. 09 31 46 81 42 | www.giuggiulena.it | Moderate*

INSIDER TIP TERRAUZZA SUL MARE ☺
This country home, run by the ceramicist Renata Emmolo, is on the Maddalena peninsula next to the sea. Organic produce. *9 flats | Via Blanco 8 | loc. Terrauzza | tel. 09 31 71 43 62 | www.terramar.it | Budget–Moderate*

VILLINO DIANA
Grand 19th-century villa on the edge of the town in a large garden with a terrace and living room with period furnishings. *5 rooms | Via Portosalvo 27 | tel. 0 93 32 11 75 | www.villinodiana.it | Budget–Moderate*

INFORMATION

STR: Via Maestranza 33 | tel. 09 31 46 42 55 | www.comune.siracusa.it

WHERE TO GO

FIUME CIANE (135 E4) *(∅ L7)*
This river, just 5km (3mi) long, comes from two rich sources in the limestone hills and enters the sea near the former salt works in Syracuse. The sources and the upper reaches of the river are the only places in Europe where papyrus sedge or paper reed occurs naturally. A 3km (1¾mi) long footpath along the river bank starts at the source on the road from Syracuse to Canicattini (7km/4½mi). One-hour● motorboat trips on the lower and middle sections of the river start at Anapo bridge on the Noto road *(2km/1¼mi) | tel. 0 93 13 98 89)*.

PANTALICA ★ (135 D4) *(∅ K7)*
Pantalica is 50km (31mi) from Syracuse via Ferla or 35km (22mi) via Sortino. A sideroad runs from both villages to the Necropolis of Pantalica created by the Sicel people. More than 5000 burial chambers from the late Neolithic period and Bronze Age, dug into the rock, line the sides of the Anapo and neighbouring valleys. They were later used as a safe refuge during turbulent periods in history. Only one villa from the 11th century BC has been excavated in the adjoining settlement. Paths at the ends of both roads link up with the river valley. Trails are signposted along the road from Ferla.

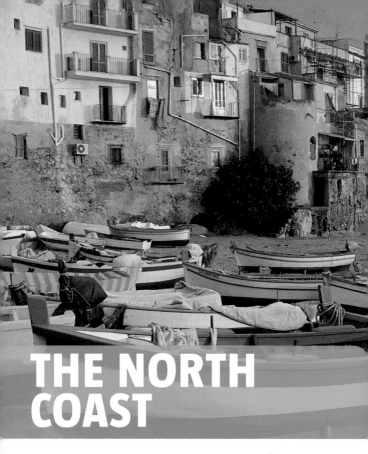

THE NORTH COAST

Craggy mountains rise immediately behind the northern coastline of Sicily. In only a few places have rivers carved out plains where the luxuriant orange plantations provide a stark contrast to the bare rock. The jagged plateaus of the foreland became the perfect hideout of the Mafia. The sea has formed wide bays enclosed by promontories, such as the Gulf of Castellammare, the Gulf of Palermo and the broad Gulf of Termini Imerese, whose boundary is marked by the rock above Cefalù. This adjoins the long stretch of coast that lies at the foot of the Madonie and Nebrodi mountains that have since been made into regional natural parks.

CEFALÙ

(131 D2) (∅ G3) The Norman cathedral with its towers and high nave look like a toy set against the rocky mountain.

The roofs of the houses are clustered around the landmark of this town (pop. 14,500) that was a burial place in the early Norman period and had a brief heyday as an important harbour before falling into a deep sleep like Sleeping Beauty until the 20th century. This left the medieval town virtually unaltered. The *Corso Ruggero*, the main street lined with austere palaces with pointed arched windows, opens onto

Photo: The Old Town in Cefalù

The lively, exhausting metropolis of Palermo, surrounded by nature reserves, dominates the north coast

the cathedral square. The Old Town is narrow and dark; a huge wall, protects the town from the sea. To the west of the Old Town is a large bay with a promenade.

SIGHTSEEING

ARABIAN WASH HOUSE

In the middle of the Old Town is a small square that leads to a row of stone basins under low arches where several springs emerge. The wash house, dating from the Arabian era, was used until just a few decades ago by the local women.

CEFALÙ CATHEDRAL ★

The impressive plain arches of the portico and the two massive towers can be seen well from the square. The stones of this, the oldest Norman cathedral in Sicily (begun

CEFALÙ

Fiumara d'Arte: an 18m (59ft) high sculpture in the Tusa valley

in 1140) and only completed after hundreds of years, speak volumes: the archaic cloisters, the bold apse and the narrow transept all symbolise strength and power. *Daily 7am–7pm*

MUSEO MANDRALISCA
Private collection of archeological finds and paintings including the famous portrait of an unknown man by Antonello da Messina. *Daily 9am–7pm | Via Mandralisca 13 | entrance fee 5 euros | www.museomandralisca.it*

INSIDER TIP ▶ LA ROCCA ⚘
La Rocca towers 268m above the town, its vertical walls protecting it from being conquered. The only access is by passing through a number of walls and gateways from Antiquity and the Middle Ages. Flights of steps and paths lead to cisterns, ruins of buildings and a pre-Roman temple in the Cyclopean style. Remember to take water with you and wear stout shoes.

FOOD & DRINK

BRACE
Imaginatively prepared pasta, vegetarian, fish and meat dishes. *Closed Mon | Via XXV Novembre 10 | tel. 09 21 42 35 70 | Moderate*

CAFFÈ LETTERARIO LA GALLERIA
Right next to the cathedral. Bar and restaurant with snacks, newspapers, a gallery, Internet access and exhibitions. *Closed Wed | Via Mandralisca 23 | tel. 09 21 42 02 11 | www.lagalleriacefalu.it | Budget*

BEACHES & SPORTS

Beautiful natural beaches can be found in *Mazzaforno* (5km/3mi to the west), in *Capo Caldura* (2km/1¼mi to the east) and in *Capo Raisigerbi* near Finale di Pollina (131 E2) *(ᗰ G3)*. Riding is available 2km (1¼mi) in the direction of Gratteri at *Fattoria Pianetti (tel. 09 21 42 18 90 | www.fattoriapianetti.com)*.

WHERE TO STAY

KALURA ⚘
Sports hotel above the cliffs, 2km (1¼mi) to the east. Terrace with panoramic views, swimming platform, pebbly beach, mountainbiking, diving. *65 rooms | Loc. Caldura | tel. 09 21 42 13 54 | www.hotel-kalura.com | Moderate–Expensive*

PALAZZO VILLELMI ⚘
B & B in the Old Town, roof terrace. *3 rooms | Corso Ruggero 149 | tel. 09 21 42 23 54 | www.palazzovillelmi.com | Budget–Moderate*

INFORMATION

STR: Corso Ruggero 77 | tel. 09 21 42 14 58 or 09 21 42 10 50

WHERE TO GO

FIUMARA D'ARTE ● (131 E2) *(𝄞 H3–4)*
Fiumara di Tusa, the beach at *Villa Margi* and *Castel di Lucio* with its maze are an open-air museum of modern scultpure. Artists also designed the rooms of the avant-garde hotel *Atelier sul Mare* (44 rooms | tel. 09 21 33 42 95 | www.atelier sulmare.com | *Expensive*) in the coastal village *Castel di Tusa* (32km/20mi) east of Cefalù). The hotel's website guides you to INSIDER TIP nine sculptures in the countryside.

🙂 *Agriturismo Casa Migliaca* is located on a hill above the Fiumara di Tusa valley near *Pettineo*. The 17th-century manorial farm-house has 8 rooms; the food (residents only) comes from its own organic produc-tion *(tel. 09 21 33 67 22 | www.casamigliaca. com | Moderate, restaurant Budget)*.

Colourful ceramics are made in ● *St Stefano di Camastra*. Most shops display their wares on the road.

MADONIE ★
(130–131 C–E2) *(𝄞 G–H4)*
You can get to know the Madonie Moun-tains by taking this circular tour (approx. 145km/90mi). The pilgrim church in *Gibilmanna* is in a holm oak wood on the edge of the mountains. Refreshing springs and paths for hiking and riding attract lots of people from the towns at the week-ends. There are also a number of good trattorias in the villages as well as places that sell cheese, local cold meats, farm-house bread, olive oil and wine. Accom-modation is available in mountain cabins and on farms *(agriturismo)*.

The mountain village INSIDER TIP *Isnello* is the gateway to what is Sicily's most important skiing area after Mount Etna. Mountain hikes of all degrees of difficulty can be made from spring until late au-tumn. *Piano Zucchi* (1105m/3625ft) and *Piano Battaglia* (1500m/4920ft), which both have cabins and hotels, are the best starting points. Just below, in a restored country house, is the *Piano Torre* hotel (26 rooms | tel. 0 92 16 26 71 | www.piano torreparkhotel.com | *Moderate*) with a pool and good restaurant. The *Rifugio Orestano* (81 beds | tel. 09 21 66 21 59 | www.rifugio restano.com | *Budget*) is simpler and well known for its authentic cooking.

From Petralia head east to *Gangi* (pop. 7000) where the closely built houses cover the mountain like a hat. The labyrinth of narrow streets can only be explored on foot. Simple accommodation and food can be found at 🙂 *Casale Villa Rainò*, 4km

(2½mi) from the town, where traditional ● *caponata,* aubergine rolls and lamb and pork from its own organic farm are served *(5 rooms | tel. 09 21 64 46 80 | www. villaraino.it | Budget).*

Now drive back 9km (5½mi) to Bivio Geraci and, from there, up to *Geraci Siculo* that lies 1077m (3530ft) above sea level. One of the most far-reaching views over Sicily is the reward for taking a walk through the narrow streets to the church and the ruins of the ☆ castle above the village. On a clear day, Etna 75km (46mi) away, looms like a giant above the barren mountainous and hilly countryside of central Sicily. There is always a lot going on at the entrance to the village around the old ● *village fountain* of pink stone. Locals as well as others from further afield come here to fill up their bottles and canisters with mineral water from a nearby spring. A twisty mountain road leads for 23km (14mi) through cork oak woods to *Castelbuono* (pop. 9200). The entrance to the Old Town is guarded by the well-preserved castle with its impressive courtyard, a museum exhibiting works by classical modern Italian painters, and the *Cappella Sant'Anna,* a masterpiece of Baroque stucco art *(Tue– Sun 8.30am–2pm, 2.30pm–8pm | entrance fee 3 euros).* The natural history museum, the *Museo Minà Palumbo,* is the life's work of the scientist Francesco Minà Palumbo, who walked the Madonie Mountains time and again in the 19th century. The showcases display snails, fossils, butterflies, hand-drawn and coloured sheets of plants, archeological finds and stuffed birds *(Mon– Sat 9am–1pm, 3pm–7pm | entrance fee 2 euros | Via Roma 52 | www.museomina palumbo.it).* INSIDER**TIP** *Nangalarruni (closed Wed | Via delle Confraternità 5 | tel. 09 21 67 14 28 | Moderate)* serves excellent country food. The *Fiasconaro* bar on the *piazza* has the best *panettone* anywhere south of Milan as well as ice cream.

PALERMO

MAP INSIDE BACK COVER
(130 B1) *(ⓜ E3)* **The location of the city (pop. 657,000) on the edge of the fertile plain, la Conca d'Oro – 'the Golden Shell' – and framed by the mountains behind Monreale and Monte Pellegrino, is magnificent. In the 18th-century the setting was even famously described as 'the most beautiful in the world'.**

Even today, the most evocative way to approach Palermo is by ship. First you catch a glimpse of the theatrical mountains on the north coast before entering the bay, where the towers and domes become increasingly clear. The centre of this, one of the most magnificent cities of palaces in Europe 200 years ago, is frequently a jolting juxtaposition of utter neglect and exuberant vitality. Parts of the Old Town are in ruins and there are still swathes of destruction where World War II bombs and subsequent speculation have torn holes in the city's fabric. This is in stark contrast to the colourful and exotic markets and other streets which are so full of people from dawn until well into the night that you

CITY WHERE TO START?
Centre: Palermo's centre and the Old Town stretch around the inner-city bay La Cala. By car, simply follow signs to the harbour (*porto*) where you can find somewhere to park in the Via Crispi or in the roads behind (pay and display). Take the Via Crispi as far as La Cala and you'll find yourself in the middle of Old Palermo. From the station (*Stazione Centrale*), which is also where most coaches stop, the Via Roma leads directly through the centre.

can hardly make headway. Life is gradually coming back to every district now. Restoration work and building is going on everywhere; committed young people are moving back into the Old Town. Shops, pubs and places to meet are opening up on every corner.

As everywhere in Sicily, the dominant architectural style is Baroque. However, the magnificence of the Norman buildings and mosaics stopped later generations from demolishing, remodelling or covering them up. On the other hand there is nothing left from earlier eras – of the hundreds of houses of worship and mosques in the city constructed by the Arabs or of the Byzantine buildings. Nevertheless, early Norman churches such as *San Giovanni degli Eremiti* and *San Cataldo* as well as to two garden palaces *La Cuba* and *La Zisa* give some impression of the Arabian influence in Sicily.

Palermo Cathedral, the burial place of royal and imperial families

SIGHTSEEING

CATTEDRALE

Only the dimensions of the cathedral and the Norman architecture of the unaltered choir are remnants of when the building was first erected (1185). The impressive Late Gothic side façade with the main portico is of Catalan influence; the dome and the interior are from the late 18th century – very sobre and austere. Inside, the polished porphyry sarcophagi of Frederick II (1194–1250) and other members of the royal and imperial families can be seen. *Cathedral daily 7am–5.30pm, royal tombs Mon–Sat 9.30am–1.30pm and 2.30pm–5.30pm | entrance fee 2 euros*

CONVENTO DEI CAPPUCCINI

Coachloads of tourists head for the Via Cappuccini in the east of the city – more than to any other cultural site in Palermo. The Capuchin friars and members of the aristocracy had themselves mummified to highlight the transitoriness of this world. Covered with dust and dressed in clothes that have become cocoons, they remain preserved in the monastery catacombs. In centuries past they were even dressed in new fashionable clothes from time to time. *Mon–Sat 9am–1pm and 3pm–5pm, Sun 9am–1pm | entrance fee 3 euros*

GALLERIA D'ARTE MODERNA

Art from between 1800 and 1900 when Palermo advanced to become a cultural metropolis for 20 years. An excellent collection of works, largely by Sicilian artists who later fell into oblivion. Around 400 works from the Classicist and Romantic periods, the 19th century, Art Nouveau and Neorealist styles are displayed in the beautifully restored former monastery of *Santa Anna alla Kalsa*. *Tue–Sun 9.30am–6.30pm | Piazza Sant'Anna ai Lattarini | entrance fee 7 euros*

PALERMO

GALLERIA REGIONALE DELLA SICILIA

Housed in the Gothic Catalan *Palazzo Abatellis,* the museum showcases Sicily's artistic past including the bust of Eleonora d'Aragon by Francesco Laurana, the head of a boy by Antonello Gaginis, and paintings on panel such as **INSIDER TIP** Antonello da Messina's 'Annunciation'. The filmmaker Wim Wenders once commented that this small picture is 'more beautiful and magical than the Mona Lisa.' *Mon–Sun 9am–1pm | Via Alloro | entrance fee 8 euros*

LA KALSA

Al-Halisah, 'the Chosen One' is the name the Arabs gave this district on the shore and around the harbour. It was here that the palace of the Caliphs once stood. Later, the nobility built palaces and churches here, enjoyed an evening walk around the *Porta Felice* and along the sea where, today, there are lots of stalls selling fish and ice cream. There is a wonderful view of the coastline and the Old Town from the **INSIDER TIP** *Passeggiata delle Cattive,* that runs along the city walls past the mighty Palazzo Butera. Following air raids in 1943, the district suffered from neglect and depopulation as a result of the Mafia and speculation. However, in the past few years, La Kalsa has experienced a revival. The *Piazza Marina* with its huge 200-year-old rubber trees and masses of trattorias is a lively spot well into the night. Lots of restoration and rebuilding work is going on in the two main streets, *Via Alloro* and *Via Torremuzza*, lined with tall Baroque palaces and churches. The façade of *San Francesco d'Assisi*, with its richly decorated rose window and portal, is impressive. The clear architectural style of the Gothic hall church is one of the few medieval churches in Palermo without any Baroque embellishments. It is a space of meditation and reflection. The life-sized plasterwork allegories of virtues and vices by Giacomo Serpotta of 1723 provide a stark contrast. A visit to *Palazzo Mirto* provides a glimpse of upper-class life in the 18th-century *(Via Merlo 2 | daily 9am–7pm | entrance fee 5 euros)*. *La Magione*, a plain Norman church with an enchanting cloister in a small park borders large open areas in this part of La Kalsa that was never rebuilt after the war *(daily 9.30am–6.30pm | entrance fee 2 euros)*.

LA MARTORANA AND SAN CATALDO

The two churches stand on a small hillock not far from the *Piazza Pretoria*. No ornamentation distracts from the plain stone structure of *San Cataldo* with its a tall red dome that has been so well preserved. The bell tower of *La Martorana* with its delicate-looking columns and pointed arched windows, became the template for many Norman churches including several in the south of mainland Italy. The interior is covered in golden mosaics by Byzantine master craftsmen. *Mon–Sat 8.30am–1pm and 3.30pm–7pm, Sun 8.30am–1pm | free entrance (La Martorana), 2 euros (San Cataldo)*

MUSEO ARCHEOLOGICO

The museum is housed in a former monastery. Burial stelae and sarcophagi are displayed in the Renaissance cloister. The ancient metopes (reliefs on a temple frieze) from Selinunt are considered to be exceptional examples of Greek sculpture. Artefacts from Antiquity and ceramics can be seen on the first floor. *Tue–Fri 8.30am–12.30pm and 3pm–6.30pm, Sat/Sun 8.30am–1.30pm | entrance fee 4 euros | Piazza Olivella*

VIA VALVERDE ORATORIES AND CHURCHES

Just a few yards apart, hidden behind the massive Baroque church of San Domenico,

The huge Fontana Pretoria outside Palermo's Town Hall

are a number of small Baroque churches and oratories. *Oratorio del Rosario* and *Oratorio di Santa Cita* contain exceptionally life-like plasterwork figures and reliefs by the Baroque artist Giacomo Serpotta; the churches *Santa Cita, Santa Maria di Valverde* and *San Giorgio dei Genovesi* have an unusual number of paintings, marble statues and stone intarsia work. *Mon–Sat 9am–1pm | entrance fee 5 euros | www.tesoridellaloggia.it*

INSIDER TIP ORTO BOTANICO (BOTANIC GARDEN) ●

Laid out as a pleasure garden in 1792 for the upper classes, the garden today is a shady paradise with huge trees from both the Mediterranean and the Tropics. It provides an extensive overview of the regional flora and those plants from all over the world that have become established here. *March/Oct daily 9am–6pm, Apr/Sept daily 9am–7pm, May–Aug daily 9am–8pm, Nov–Feb Mon–Sat 9am–5pm, Sun 9am–2pm | Via Lincoln | entrance fee 5 euros | www.ortobotanico.palermo.it*

INSIDER TIP PALAZZINA CINESE

200 years ago, everything Chinese was considered the height of fashion. In 1790 the Bourbon kings had a residence built and finished in the Chinese style in Favorita Park. *Tue–Sat 10am–6pm, Sun 9am–1.30pm | Parco della Favorita half way to Mondello | entrance fee 6 euros*

PALAZZO DEI NORMANNI AND THE CAPPELLA PALATINA ★

The former *royal palace*, the origins of which date back to the 9th century, has been the seat of the regional government of Sicily and regional parliament since 1947. The *cappella*, the royal chapel, was embellished by Arab, Norman and Byzantine artists. The interior is completely covered with gold mosaics and marble intarsia, the former being the work of artists from Constantinople. The chancel contains King Roger II's coronation throne with rich intarsia work, the Easter candlestick, the ambon used as a pulpit and the high altar. The wooden 'stalactite' ceiling, which can now be seen in all its colourful magnificence following its restoration, looks as if it has come out of an Oriental fairy tale. The entrance is outside the city wall. *Mon–Sat 8.15am–5.45pm, Sun 8.15am–1pm (not during mass 9.45am–11.15am) | Piazza Indipendenza | entrance fee 7, with a tour guide (Sat–Mon) 8.50 euros | tel. for reservations 09 16 26 28 33*

SAN GIOVANNI DEGLI EREMITI

In the garden of the former monastery church below the Norman palace, the sound of water, the palm trees and exotic plants give a very good idea of the opulence of oriental Palermo and the Arab-influenced lifestyle led by the privileged in Norman times, to which the monks of certain monasteries also belonged. *Tue–Sun 9am–6.30pm | entrance fee 6 euros*

TEATRO MASSIMO ●

This is one of the most important classicist buildings in Sicily, designed by the architect Giovan B. Basile of Palerma and erected in 1875–97. After the opera houses in Paris and Vienna, it is the largest in Europe. *Opera season Nov–May, Tue–Sun 10am–2.30pm | Piazza Verdi | 5 euros | www.teatromassimo.it*

INSIDER TIP LA ZISA

In the 12th century, Arabian builders erected this royal summer residence. The tall cube is elegantly subdivided by decorative arches, windows and portals. The fountain niche, with its delicate pendant arches, and from which the water originally flowed outside, can be seen in the imposing hall decorated with mosaic friezes and marble tiles. Concealed flues, clay pipes and running water created a form of air conditioning that still works 800 years on. *Tue–Sun 9am–6.30pm | entrance fee 6 euros*

FOOD & DRINK

INSIDER TIP ANTICA FOCACCERIA SAN FRANCESCO

Take-away and pizzeria, with pretty Art Deco furnishings, self service, tables on the lovely Piazza San Francesco available if you have a full meal. *Closed Tue | Via A. Paternostro 58 | tel. 0 91 32 03 64 | Budget*

CASCINARI

The traditional dishes served in this trattoria near the flea market are popular among students, sales staff, workers and managers alike. *Closed Mon | Via D'Ossuna 43 | tel. 09 16 51 98 04 | Budget*

KURSAAL KALHESA

Restaurant, pub and bookshop under one roof in the middle of the up-and-coming Kalsa district where heated debates and Sicilian food are enjoyed. *Closed Mon | Foro Umberto 21 | tel. 09 16 16 22 82 | www.kursaalkalhesa.it | Moderate*

MAESTRO DEL BRODO

Once a mundane soup kitchen, now much more elegant. Apart from soups and meat dishes, pasta, vegetables and fish are also served. *Closed Mon | Via Pannieri 7 | Vucciria | tel. 0 91 32 95 23 | Moderate*

INSIDER TIP IL MIRTO E LA ROSA ☺

Fresh seasonal produce, lots of vegetarian, seafood and a few meat dishes from naturally reared animals, exquisite desserts. *Via Principe di Granatelli 30 | tel. 0 91 32 53 53 | www.ilmirtoelarosa.com | Moderate*

SANTANDREA

Well-known for its fish. In summer, there are also tables outside on the square. Evenings only. *Closed Sun | Piazza Sant'Andrea 4 | tel. 0 91 33 49 99 | Moderate*

SHOPPING

CRAFT SHOPS

The district between the *station*, *Via Roma, Piazza Cassa di Risparmio, Piazza Rivoluzione* and *Via Garibaldi* is a piece of 'Old Palermo' with craftspeople such as milliners, tailors and candlemakers.

LA COPPOLA STORTA ●

This is where you can buy a genuine Sicilan *coppala* from San Giuseppe Jato, in any number of colours, for men, women and children, made of coarse or soft material, and for every conceivable occasion. And just to rid any doubt as to who wears this cap today: the shop is on the 'Addiopizzo' list. *Via Bara all'Olivella 74*

STREET MARKETS ★ ●

There are several food markets in the Old Town. And, after a lengthy midday break, the standholders keep going well into the evening. The largest *market in the Capo district* is held around Sant'Agostino church and stretches down several roads as far as the Teatro Massimo; the *Ballaró-Markt* caters for the area around Porta Sant'Antonio, the Chiesa del Carmine and Chiesa del Gesù. The biggest *non-food market*, consisting largely of clothing and household wares, sprawls through the Old Town from Piazza San Domenico to Piazza Papireto. The famous *Vucciria market* between Via Roma and the harbour is also going to be given a new lease of life.

WHERE TO STAY

The majority of basic hotels are used as permanent accommodation, many are run-down and dirty.

CENTRALE PALACE

A small, historical, 'grand' hotel, recently renovated. *104 rooms | Corso Vittorio*

Don't miss a visit to one of Palermo's lively markets

Emanuele 327 | tel. 0 91 33 66 66 | www. centralepalacehotel.it | Expensive

FUMBI

This modern B & B, with non-smoking rooms only, is in the Libertà district. *4 rooms | Via Generale Arimondi 48 | tel. 09 16 76 05 53 | www.fumbi.com | Budget*

JOLI

Turn-of-the-century building on the Piazza Ignazio Florio with bold colours and wall and ceiling frescos. Roof terrace. *30 rooms | Via Michele Amari 11 | tel. 09 16 11 17 65 | www.hoteljoli.com | Moderate*

TONIC

Grand early 20th-century building, in a peaceful and central location. *36 rooms | Via Mariano Stabile 126 | tel. 0 91 58 17 54 | www.hoteltonic.it | Budget–Moderate*

APT: Piazza Castelnuovo 34 | tel. 09 16 05 83 51 | www.palermotourism.com (for both the city and the region) and www.palermoweb.com, www.comune.palermo.it/comune/assessorato_turismo (for the city only)

WHERE TO GO

BAGHERIA (130 B1) (*Ⅲ F3*)

In the 18th and 19th centuries, the splendid villas, gardens and parks of the foremost aristocratic families could be found close to this town (pop. 56,000), 16km (10mi) east of Palermo. The *Villa Palagonia*, with its array of sculpted monsters in the garden, its hall of mirrors and the frescos of the Labours of Hercules inside *(daily 9am–1pm, April–Oct 4pm–7pm, Nov–March 3.30pm–5.30pm | entrance fee 5 euros | www.villapalagonia.it)* aroused the curiosity of a number of illustrious travellers such as John Soane and Alexandre Dumas. The Neorealist painter Renato Guttuso (1911–87) set up the *Galleria d'Arte Moderna* in the *Villa Cattolica* where he displayed his own works alongside those of other 20th-century Sicilian artists *(daily summer 9.30am–2pm, 3pm–7.30pm, winter 9am–1pm, 2.30pm–7pm | entrance fee 5 euros | www.museoguttuso.com). Trattoria Don Ciccio* serves good old fashioned fare *(closed Wed, Sun and in August | Budget).*

CORLEONE (130 B3) (*Ⅲ E4*)

This small town (pop. 11,000), the home of bosses and godfathers, crops up in virtually every Mafia novel and nearly every related film, as well as in daily reports in the press and on television, even though the 'Corleonesi' didn't actually reach any positions of power within the Mafia through bloody means until they were in Palermo. In the 😊 INSIDER TIP *Casa della Legalità* in the town centre, once in the ownership of the former superboss Provenzano and impounded by the State, photos and pictures of Gaetano Porcasi can be seen as well as documents about the Mafia and the struggle against the godfathers. Produce and wine grown on land seized from Mafia clans is also sold here *(Mon–Thu 9.30am–1.30pm | Cortile Colletti | www.laboratoriodellalegalita.it).*

The craggy bastion, the INSIDER TIP *Rocca Busambra,* lies 1613m (4318ft) above sea level in barren hilly country. The mountain forests, caves and clefts in this karst landscape provided perfect hiding and burial places for the Mafia. Some of these can be reached along waymarked trails which start at *Bosco di Ficuzza,* the former hunting lodge of Bourbon kings. Accommodation and good food is available at *Alpe Cucco*, a mountain hotel easily reached by car which lies at an altitude of just under 1000m *(18 rooms | 102 beds | tel. 09 18 20 82 25 | www.alpecucco.it | Budget).*

MONDELLO (130 B1) (*Ⅲ E3*)

'Palermo's' beach is 15km (9½mi) from the city, protected from the worst of the

Heaven on earth: the golden mosaics in Monreale Cathedral

pollution by Monte Pellegrino. Some of the Art Nouveau villas with their beautiful gardens have not yet been hemmed in by concrete blocks. The modern *Splendid Hotel La Torre (166 rooms | tel. 0 91 45 02 22 | Moderate–Expensive)* lies above the Tyrrhenian Sea; *Conchiglia d'Oro (50 rooms | tel. 0 91 45 03 59 | Moderate)* is on a quiet side road. The restaurant *Bye Bye Blues (closed Tue | Via Garofalo 23 | tel. 09 16 84 14 15 | Moderate)* has excellent seafood.

MONREALE (130 B1) (*ℳ E3*)
The ★ *Cathedral of Monreale (8km/5mi west of Palermo)* was founded as a Benedictine monastery in 1174 under the Normans and granted a huge area of land, taking in the whole of western Sicily. It is the largest and most compact ecclesiastical building on the island. Inside, approached through two Roman bronze doors, the walls are completely covered in golden mosaics covering 68,250ft² *(April–Oct*

daily 8am–6pm, Nov–March daily 8am–12.30pm and 3.30pm–6pm). The flora and fauna ornamentation on the capitals in the ● cloister *(daily 9am–7pm | entrance fee 6 euros)*, arranged around a garden with a fountain, introduces a natural element into the secluded world of the monastery. A little outside the town, with a panoramic view, is the hotel ≋ *Carrubella Park (30 rooms | tel. 09 16 40 21 88 | Moderate)*. Sicilian country fare can be enjoyed on the cathedral square in *Bricco & Bracco (closed Mon | Via D'Acquisto 13 | tel. 09 16 41 77 73 | Moderate)*.

MONTE PELLEGRINO ★ ≋ (130 B1) (*ℳ E3*)
Palermo's 'own' thickly wooded mountain is 13km (8mi) from the city and 606m (1990ft) high, and offers a fantastic view over the city and the Conca d'Oro. The sanctuary dedicated to St Rosalia, the patron saint of Palermo, is built in a natural cave.

THE SOUTHWEST

The west and south coast between Gela and Selinunte are largely untouched by tourism. Only not-to-be-missed sites such as the Greek temples in Agrigento, Selinunte and Segesta experience hordes of visitors.

To the north between Trapani and Alcamo, bare mountains mark the boundary of the expansive plains with their salt works and endless vineyards stretching as far as Marsala and Selinunte on the south coast. This links up with an also seemingly endless expanse of undulating mountainous and hilly countryside with wide valleys and villages perched on mountain tops. Following the brief but intense period in early summer when everything bursts into life, when poppies and gorse blossom and fields of crops turn red and yellow, the vitually treeless ground becomes scorched almost everywhere, its once sparse woodland having fallen victim to the axe more than 2000 years ago.

AGRIGENTO

(130 C5) (*Ⓜ F6*) The ancient Greek city of Akragas, the medieval Girgenti and the Agrigento of the past 30 years are three towns that, unlike other places in Sicily, are not built one on top of the other.

Photo: 'Tempel C', Selinunte

From the obligatory tours of ancient sites to unchartered tourist territory: ruined temples, endless vineyards and bizarre rock formations

Each has its own site, even if the high-rises in new Agrigento (pop. 59,000) partially block the view of Old Girgenti and the city from Antiquity in the *Valle dei Templi*.

SIGHTSEEING

OLD TOWN

The urban centre is the *Piazzale Aldo Moro* with its many palm trees that links the medieval part with the modern town. Both from here and the ☆ park along the *Viale della Vittoria* you have a fantastic panoramic view across the Valley of the Temples and the sea.

On the *Via Atenea*, take the first flight of steps – that are so typical of Girgenti – up to the church of *Santo Spirito*. In the *Chiesa del Purgatorio* on Via Atenea there is a splendid INSIDER TIP cycle of figures

These columns in the Temple of Heracles are more than 10m (33ft) high

telamon from the Temple of Olympian Zeus can be seen in one of the rooms. The Romanesque monastery church of *San Nicola*, where the Phaedra sarcophagus from Late Antiquity depicting the tragic love of Phaedra and her stepson Hippolytus can be seen, also belongs to the museum. *Tue–Sat 9am–7.30pm, Sun/Mon 9am–1.30pm | entrance fee 8 euros, incl. excavations 10 euros*

VALLE DEI TEMPLI ★

The ancient city and its temples lie hidden among well-tended almond and olive groves. Start your tour from the centre of the plateau taking the usual approach along road no. 118. To the left, a path leads to the piles of stones of the *Temple of Heracles* of which only 8 columns are still standing. A small museum has been created in *Villa Aurea*. You then have an unrestricted view of the impressively symetrical Temple of Concorde from the 5th century BC. Its exceptional condition is due to its conversion into a Christian church in the 6th century. After taking the path to the *Temple of Juno*, which has half its original columns still standing, located at the highest point of ancient Akragas, walk directly above the steep drop and look down on the *Tomb of Theron*.

Returning to the car park, you enter the archeological zone. The *Temple of Olympian Zeus* is a pile of huge blocks of stone and column drums. Building work started following the victory over the Carthaginians at Himera in 480 BC. With a length of 112m (367ft) and a width of 58m (190ft), it was one of the largest temples in Antiquity. The Carthaginians destroyed the incomplete building in 406 BC and it was later further damaged by an earthquake. At the far boundary of the lower level with remains of a holy site, is the *Sanctuary of the Chtonic Gods (Tempio delle divinità chtonie)* with sacrificial pits and the *Temple*

of the virtues by Giacomo Serpotta (caretaker in courtyard). The *cathedral* is on the highest point of the Old Town. Its large, bright interior with octagonal pillars and richly carved coffered ceiling is impressive.

MUSEO ARCHEOLOGICO REGIONALE

Finds from ancient Akragas and the early culture of various peoples in the centre of Sicily. A model of the 7.75m (25½ft) high

of Castor and Pollux. A path leads down to the INSIDER TIP Giardino della Kolymbetra (daily 10am–6pm | entrance fee 2 euros), a natural paradise with orange groves, almond and olive treees. Galleries in the sandstone walls lead to subterranean springs whose water was used to irrigate the valley and for fish farming. *Daily 8.30am–7pm | entrance fee 8 euros, incl. museum 10 euros | www.parcovalledei templi.it*

Don't forget to take plenty of water with you as well as some *panini* and fruit for a picnic if you visit the very extensive and sunny *Zona Archeologica*. Eating out in Agrigento and in the Valle dei Templi, regardless of the restaurant category, is one of the worst in Sicily with regard to value for money.

FOOD & DRINK

DA CARMELO
Snails, rabbit, lamb and kid are served in this village trattoria. *Closed Wed | Joppolo Giancaxio | 12km (7½mi) north | Via Roma 16 | tel. 09 22 63 13 76 | Budget*

GIOVANNI
Fish and vegetable dishes in pleasant surroundings in the Old Town. *Closed Sun | Piazza Vadalà | tel. 0 92 22 11 10 | Moderate*

WHERE TO STAY

Most hotels are in the new Villaggio Mosè suburb. Accommodation in the Old Town and in the Valle dei Templi should be booked well in advance.

AGRITURISMO FATTORIA MOSÈ ☺
17th-century manor house and organic farm, garden and museum. *8 flats | Villaggio Mosè | Via Mattia Pascal 4 | tel. 09 22 60 61 15 | www.fattoriamose.com | Moderate*

BAGLIO DELLA LUNA ☼
In the listed gentleman's house on a wine-growing estate in the Valle dei Templi with a lovely view of ancient Akragas. *23 rooms | Contrada Maddalusa | tel. 09 22 51 10 61 | www.bagliodellaluna.com | Expensive*

VILLA CETTA (130 C6) (ル F6)
B & B with garden on the beach in San Leone. *2 rooms | Via Giovanni Fattori 9 | tel. 09 22 41 64 52 | www.villacetta.it | Budget–Moderate*

INFORMATION

STR: Via Empedocle 73 | tel. 0 92 22 03 91

WHERE TO GO

INSIDER TIP ▶ CAMPOBELLO DI LICATA
(131 D6) (*ω G6*)

Since 1980, the Argentinian artist Silvio Benedetto has been designing squares, decorating façades with murals, sculpting and creating wall and floor mosaics in this former mining town (pop. 11.500). In the *Valle delle Pietre dipinte*, characters and scenes from Dante's *Divine Comedy* have been depicted on 110 travertine slabs *(Tue–Sun 9am–1pm, 3pm–6pm | free entrance)*. Scenes and figures from Homer's *Iliad* on 24 ceramic tiles create one large image (7 × 3m, 23 × 10ft) in the auditorium. Further information under: *www.comune. campobellodilicata.ag.it* and *www.silvio benedetto.com*

GELA
(134 A4) (*ω H7*)

This industrial town (pop. 77,000) 78km (48½mi) east of Agrigento is worth a detour to see the Greek town walls at *Capo Soprano*. In keeping with Gela's importance in Antiquity, the *Museo Regionale Archeologico* next to the Parco Rimembranza

(daily 9am–6.30pm | entrance fee 4 euros) boasts a number of valuable finds and a remarkable coin collection. The trattoria *San Giovanni (closed Sun | Via da Maggio Fischetti 51 | tel. 09 33 91 26 74 | Budget)* has good meat and pasta dishes. The beach in *Falconara*, 20km (12½mi) towards Agrigento, with a castle in the background, is lovely.

PALMA DI MONTECHIARO
(130 C6) (*ω F6*)

The family of the novelist Giuseppe Tomasi di Lampedusa originated from this town 24km (15mi) east of Agrigento. *Marina di Palma* is just 4km (2½mi) away where the cliffs are dominated by a ruined castle. One of the most creative cuisines in Sicily, INSIDER TIP ▶ *La Madia (closed Tue | Via Filippo Re 22 | tel. 09 22 77 14 43 | www. ristorantelamadia.it | Expensive)*, can be found in the port of *Licata* 18km (11mi) away. Those who want to spend less but still want to enjoy culinary delights of often surprising ingenuity, head for *L'Oste e il Sacrestano (closed Sun evening and in Oct. | Via S Andrea 19 | tel. 09 22 77 46 36 | Moderate)* in the centre.

REALMONTE AND SICULIANA
(130 B5) (*ω E6*)

Between Porto Empedocle and Sciacca the main road runs 3–8km (2–5mi) inland from the coast with smaller roads leading off to secluded beaches. Near Realmonte, snow-white sandstone cliffs at *Capo Rosello* drop 90m into the sea below. Apart from a rocky coastline, *Siciliana Marina* has a flat sandy beach that stretches to the west as far as Torre Salsa.
La Scogliera on the promenade along the shore serves good seafood *(closed Mon | tel. 09 22 81 75 32 | Moderate)*. Accommodation is available in holiday flats and in the hotel *Paguro Residence (12 rooms | tel. 09 22 81 55 12 | Budget–Moderate)* in the

LOW BUDGET

▶ Unrefined sea salt from the *Ettore Infersa* pits on Mozia makes a nice souvenir – the packaging alone is a delight *(to the west of the Marsala–Birgi road | www.salineettoreinfersa. com/home.html)*.

▶ *Antichi Sapori: Mamma* is personally in charge of the cooking in this simple but good restaurant in Partanna. *Via Vittorio Emanuele 211 | tel. 09 24 92 26 18*

town above the beach. The INSIDER TIP dunes at *Torre Salsa* line the 6km (4mi) long beach and form part of the WWF nature reserve that covers 1880 acres *(entrance at the visitor centre | tel. 32 86 36 75 84 | www.wwftorresalsa.it)*. The *agriturismo* farm *Torre Salsa (13 flats | tel. 09 22 84 70 74 | www.torresalsa.it | Moderate)* is located behind the dunes.

MARSALA

(128 C4) (*B4)* **Towards the west, Sicily flattens out before running into the sea. *Capo Lilibeo*, the most westerly point of the island, is part of the town of Marsala (pop. 40,000).**

Marsala is the marketing and wine centre of western Sicily, a role for which John Woodhouse is to be thanked. While under Napoleonic rule, he created Marsala fortified wine as a substitute for the much loved port so missed by the English.

It will be some time before these grapes are made into wine

SIGHTSEEING

OLD TOWN

The very pretty Baroque town lies inside the largely intact 16th-century town walls. The cheerful façades are so typical of towns in the rich agricultural west of Sicily. The *Piazza della Repubblica* is the town's front room with arcades and loggias, a fountain in the middle and the cathedral of *San Tomaso*. The foundations of the Roman settlement are beyond *Porta Nuova*.

ENOMUSEO ●

The history of the vineyard and its everyday care, together with a wine tasting. However, when coaches are parked outside, it will be very squashed within. *Daily 8.30am–1pm and 3pm–7pm | on road 115 towards Mazara | free entrance*

MUSEO ARCHEOLOGICO BAGLIO ANSELMI

The remains of a Punic ship from the 3rd century BC that was raised in 1969 off Marsala and restored can be seen here. Also includes finds from this Punic and Roman settlement and artefacts from graves. *Sun–Tue 9am–1.30pm, Wed–Sat 9am–7pm | on Capo Lilibeo | entrance fee 4 euros*

FOOD & DRINK

GARIBALDI

Trattoria in the Old Town with regional fish dishes. *Closed Sat | Piazza Addolorata 35 | tel. 09 23 95 30 06 | Budget*

SHOPPING

Wine tasting is possible in many wineries which also have direct sales.

WHERE TO STAY

ACOS

Modern hotel for overnight stays on the outskirts with good restaurant. *35 rooms | Via Mazara 14 | tel. 09 23 99 91 66 | www. acoshotel.com | Moderate*

WHERE TO GO

GIBELLINA ★ (129 E4) (*Ø D4*)

Following the earthquake in 1968, temporary shelters were built in Belice Valley that threatened to become a permanent feature. Government funding was diverted into the pockets of the Mafia and corrupt politicians. Gibellina had been devastated and the utterly demoralised residents struggled as more and more people left. They demonstrated in Rome and invited not only politicians to visit them but also artists who drew attention to Gibellina and reconstruction efforts. The old village is a sea of debris, partly overgrown and partly a concrete monument. Alberto Burri's *Cretto* is continuously growing and is thought to be the largest work of land art in Europe with regard to the area it covers. The new settlement is 20km (12½mi) away. It is an urban experiment with remarkable modern architectural designs and a pleasant and spaciously laid-out residential landscape with gardens. In the *Museo delle Trame Mediterranee* in Baglio di Stefano just outside the town, works by classical modernist and contemporary artists (Joseph Beuys, Giorgio de Chirico, Pietro Consagra, Renato Guttuso), delicate jewellery, ceramics and sumptuous garments largely from North Africa and the Orient are on display *(Tue–Sun 9am–1pm, 3pm–6pm | entrance fee 5 euros | www.orestiadi.it)*. The *Museo d'Arte Contemporanea* boasts the largest collection of modern art in Sicily, comprising 1800 paintings, statues and other objects. Village life before the earthquake is documented in the ethnological section which focuses on old professions and the equipment used. *www.comune.gibellina.*

Gibellina under cement: a monumental memorial by the artist Alberto Burri

tp.it provides a virtual tour of the 45 sculptures and architectural designs of roads and squares. B & B *Gibellina Arte (Via Empedocle 16 | tel. 0 92 46 76 97 | www. gibellinaarte.it | Budget)* has 6 rooms and a kitchen for guests.

The large ● INSIDER**TIP** spa *Terme di Acqua Pia (Tel. 0 92 53 90 26 | www.terme acquapia.it)* is situated on the road to Montevago (20km/12½mi southeast) with a pool, spa area, hot springs, park, restaurant *(Budget)* and guest accommodation *(26 rooms, 3 flats | Budget–Moderate)*.

MAZARA DEL VALLO (128 C4) (*Ⓜ C5*)

This town 22km (14mi) southeast of Marsala is Italy's largest fishing port. The Old Town is rather like a *kasbah* – white and plain, with just a few solitary palm trees towering over it. The *Piazza della Repubblica* is a beacon in the Baroque design of squares; the interior of the *cathedral* an example of the exceptional quality of Sicilian stucco craftsmanship to be able to imitate every conceivable material using plaster, gold leaf and paint. Maritime archeological finds are displayed in the *Museo del Satiro (daily 9am–6pm | Piazza Plebiscito | 6 euros)* in the former church of Sant'Egidio. The highlight is the INSIDER**TIP** dancing Satyr, a 2m (6'7'') high bronze statue from the 4th century BC. The *Mahara Hotel (81 rooms | tel. 09 23 67 38 00 | www.mahara hotel.it | Expensive)* overlooks the palm trees along the sea-front promenade. Mussel lovers head for the *Trattoria delle Cozze (Basiricò | on the coast road to Torre Granitola | tel. 09 23 94 23 23 | Budget)*.

INSIDER**TIP** ROCCHE DI CUSA ●
(129 D5) (*Ⓜ C5*)

Column drums and capitals intended for the construction of the gigantic 'Temple G' in Selinunte, which were never used, have been lying in the ancient quarry Rocche di Cusa on the edge of Campobello di Mazara for 2500 years. The long and narrow archeological area is a picturesque natural site, accessible to all and crisscrossed by a number of paths.

SANTA MARGHERITA DI BELICE
(129 E4) (*Ⓜ D5*)

The family of the writer Giuseppe Tomasi di Lampedusa owned the large palace *Filangeri Cutò* in Santa Margherita di Belice which, after being destroyed by an earthquake in 1968, was rebuilt on the same site. The palace has also been reconstructed and is now the Town Hall and literature museum *Museo del Gattopardo*, containing wax figures, books, manuscripts and photographs. Films are also screened here. *(Daily 9.30am–1pm, 2pm–7.30pm | entrance fee 3, guided tours 5 euros | www. parcotomasi.it/en*

SELINUNTE ★
(129 D5) (*Ⓜ D5*)

The Greek temples on an elevated plateau above the sea can be seen from a long way away. The columns of two temples have been reconstructed; the third is a huge pile of stones. The largest part of this ancient city, 52km (32mi) southeast of Marsala, still lies hidden in the earth. The distances within the excavation zone alone and the size of the *Acropolis* give some idea as to the dimensions of this city from Antiquity, whose heyday resulted from the wheat trade and lasted just 300 years. *Daily 9am–sunset | entrance fee 9 euros* The modern coastal resort of *Marinella* has extensive sandy beaches, especially around the mouth of the River Belice. *Alceste (26 rooms | tel. 0 92 44 61 84 | www. hotelalceste.net | Moderate)* is a pleasant tourist hotel. The restaurant *Africa (closed Thu | Via Alceste 24 | tel. 0 92 44 64 56 | Moderate)* on the sea promenade serves good and imaginative regional fare.

SCIACCA

(129 E5) *(Ⓜ D5)* **This avalanche of buildings (pop. 40,000) that tumbles down the hill to the fishing harbour looks like an oriental *kasbah*.**

The Old Town is a labyrinth only accessible on food; many streets are just wide enough for two people to pass. The flights of steps in the upper parts of the town date largely from the Arab period. The Old Town is surrounded by a wall with lovely Baroque towers. The main thoroughfare, the *Corso Vittorio Emanuele*, that runs above the steep slope down to the harbour, is lined by palatial residences and the principal churches. Locals meet for their evening *corso* on the large square in front of the Jesuite college. After passing the delightful Baroque *cathedral* you reach the municipal park and the *thermal baths*, very much in the turn-of-the-century style when the hot springs and steam fumaroles of Sciacca made it one of the major spa resorts in Europe. In the 20th-century, Filippo Bentivegna created a bizarre collection of naïve sculptures with stylised and exaggerated features. Row upon row of sculpted stone heads can now be seen in his olive grove. He bequeathed his INSIDER TIP *Castello Incantato* to the town of Sciacca *(Tue–Sun 9am–1pm and 4pm–8pm, Oct–Feb 9am–1pm and 3pm–5pm | entrance fee 3 euros | www.castelloincantato.net)*.

FOOD & DRINK

HOSTARIA DEL VICOLO

In the upper part of the Old Town, fish dishes and excellent seafood salads. *Closed Mon | Vicolo Sammaritano 10 | tel. 0 92 52 30 71 | Moderate*

Sicily's most daring location: massive rocks tower over Caltabellotta

BEACHES & SPORTS

Sandy bays that have not yet been spoilt by mass tourism can be found along the road to Agrigento: INSIDER TIP *Torre Macauda, Torre Verdura* and *Secca Grande* as well as the large nature reserve at the mouth of the Fiume Platani, that stretches as far as *Capo Bianco* below Eraclea Minoa. Secca Grande is a must for divers.

WHERE TO STAY

AGRITURISMO MONTALBANO ☺

Organic farm on the Palermo road. Pool. *4 flats | tel. 09 25 68 01 54 | www.azienda montalbano.com | Budget*

PALOMA BLANCA

This simple, clean hotel is right next to the spa. *15 rooms | Via Figuli 5 | tel. 0 92 52 56 67 | www.lapalomablanca.it | Budget–Moderate*

VILLA PALOCLA

8 rooms with period furniture in a 17th-century country house with its own restaurant. *3km (1¾mi) southeast of Sciacca | tel. 09 25 90 28 12 | www.villaplocla.it | Moderate*

INFORMATION

Via Vittorio Emanuele 84 | tel. 0 92 52 27 44 | www.servizioturisticoregionalesciacca.it

WHERE TO GO

INSIDER TIP CALTABELLOTTA ⤴
(129 F5) (*ω E5*)

Many places in Sicily have been built in daring locations but few are like Caltabellotta (19km/12mi northeast of Sciacca), below a range of cliffs with castles and churches growing out of the rock. The view, especially from the ruins of the castle which can be reached up steps, takes in a large sweep of the island.

ERACLEA MINOA ★ ⤴
(129 F6) (*ω E6*)

The snow-white chalk cliffs 33km (20½mi) southeast of Sciacca drop 80m vertically into the sea. Above, on the flat, are the remains of the ancient town. The *amphitheatre*, carved out of the soft stone, is now protected from further erosion under a Plexiglass roof *(daily 9am–sunset | entrance fee 4 euros)*. In nearby Montallegro, *Relais Briuccia* is housed in a restored former nobleman's palace. The rooms are appropriately furnished with 4-posters *(8 rooms | Via Trieste 1 | tel. 09 22 84 77 55 | www.relaisbriuccia.it | Moderate)*. The restaurant, *Capitolo Primo*, which serves imaginative seafood, is in the inner courtyard *(closed Mon | Moderate)*.

TRAPANI

MAP INSIDE BACK COVER
(128 C3) (*ω C3*) **The town (pop. 70,000) sticks out into the sea like a long finger, with 750m (2460ft)-high Mount Erice towering up behind. To the south, is an endless flat expanse with salt-pans with windmills and dazzlingly white piles of salt; the islands out to sea look like floating icebergs.**

The largely Baroque Old Town is hidden behind the elongated harbour. The Renaissance *Palazzo Riccio* has a lovely courtyard with arcades and loggias. The *Palazzo Cavarretto* with the Sicilian eagle and two clocks gracing its façade, forms the end, optically, of the *Corso Vittorio Emanuele*. The magnificent ornamentation on the Jesuite church *Chiesa del Collegio* is typical of the order.

The salt-pans outside the town are still partly in operation today. The remaining salt marsh with more than 60 windmills is a listed site.

SIGHTSEEING

MUSEO REGIONALE PEPOLI
This museum has extremely important collections of medieval and modern art. It is housed in the former convent *Santuario dell'Annunziata* and boasts works by Antonello Gagini and a painting by Titian, among others. Gold work, coral carvings and majolica pieces are testimonies to the skill of master craftsmen from Trapani. *Mon–Sat 9am–1.30pm, Sun 9am–12.30pm | entrance fee 4 euros*

FOOD & DRINK

CANTINA SICILIANA
This lively restaurant serving seafood with couscous, sea urchin, tuna and squid, is close to the harbour. *Via Giudecca 36 | tel. 0 92 32 86 73 | Moderate*

SAVERINO
On Via Lungomare in *Tonnara di Bonagia* (8km/5mi towards San Vito), tasteful design, food prepared by mother and daughters. Also has 20 rooms. *Tel. 09 23 59 27 27 | www.saverino.it | Moderate*

TRA...PANIVINI
Unusually cheap food in a wineshop in the Old Town, small snacks and good wine. *Via Carolina 42 | tel. 0 92 32 76 25 | Budget*

WHERE TO STAY

BAGLIO FONTANASALSA
Large 18th-century farm with a pool and restaurant *(Budget | reservation essential)*. *9 rooms | on road to Marsala | tel. 09 23 59 10 01 | www.fontanasalsa.it | Moderate*

NUOVO RUSSO
Well-run town hotel in the centre, close to the harbour. *35 rooms | Via Tintori 4 | tel. 0 92 32 21 66 | Moderate*

INFORMATION

STR: Via San Francesco d'Assisi 27 | tel. 09 23 54 55 07

WHERE TO GO

AEGADIAN ISLANDS (ISOLE EGADI)
(128 A–B3) *(ℳ A–B 3–4)*
Ferries and hydrofoils cross to the three islands off Trapani several times a day. The small limestone islands are surrounded by unpolluted waters; the caves and rich unterwater life attract divers in particular. *Favignana* (7½mi², 33km/21mi coastline, pop. 4300) is still one of the most important tuna fisheries today. Soft volcanic tuff was once quarried along the mostly flat rocky coastline and used in the building trade. The bizarre shapes of these quarries right on the shore can still be seen. Most of the island is flat and covered with fields with the 314m (1030ft) high *Monte Santa Caterina* rising in the middle with a fortess on the top. Bays suitable for swimming and a few sandy patches can be found in the south of the island. For accommodation and the best seafood try INSIDER TIP *Egadi (11 rooms | Via Colombo 17 | tel. 09 23 92 12 32 | www.albergoegadi. it | Moderate–Expensive)*.

Levanzo (2⅓mi², 12km/7½mi coastline, pop. 200) is a 278m (910ft) high rocky outcrop which, apart from the fields on the flat part of the island and the terraces above the harbour, is covered by thick *macchia*. The coastline is rugged and rocky. The *Grotta del Genovese* is a prehistoric site. The drawings of animals carved into the rock are approx. 12,000 years old. The wall paintings of people dancing,

The most beautiful bays and caves on Marettimo can only be reached by boat

animals and idols are some 5000 years old. The cave can be reached by boat or a 4×4 *(duration of journey/guided tour 3 hrs. | bookings under tel. 33 97 41 88 00 and 09 23 92 40 32 | www.grottadelgenovese. it)*. Simple accommodation and good fisherman's fare is available in *Paradiso (23 rooms | Lungomare | tel. 09 23 92 40 80 | Moderate)*.

INSIDER TIP *Marettimo* (4⅔mi², 19km/ 12mi coastline, pop. 700) has a cragged mountain ridge rising 686m (2250ft) out of the sea. There are only a few places where the sea can be accessed easily from the land and the marvellous bays and caves are best reached by boat (tours from the harbour). Underwater, Marettimo is a dreamworld. Hikers can follow goat paths up the eastern flank of the island to the ruined fortress *Punta Troia* and to

the lighthouse on the even more remote west coast. The Trattoria *Il Veliero (Tel. 09 23 92 32 74 | Moderate)* is the island's meeting place where you can enjoy good and hearty fish dishes. Accommodation is availabe in private homes – owners are at the harbour to meet the boats.

ERICE ⭐ 🌿 (128 C3) (*ᗐ C3*)

14km (9mi) northeast of Trapani, virtually directly above the sea at a height of 700m, is the medieval town of Erice with its grey stone houses. It is often hidden in the clouds even when the sun is blazing down on the rest of western Sicily. The Elymians and Phoenicians from Asia Minor worshipped Astarte, the goddess of love, and the Romans built a large sanctuary to Venus on the site of the present-day *Norman castle*. Although the town is largely deserted, it doesn't show the otherwise so obvious signs of decay as it is the place many Sicilians come to at the weekend to enjoy the cooler air. The view over the plains and salt-pans, the islands in the shallow sea off Marsala, the Aegadian Islands and the rocky coastline of San Vito is quite exceptional. The quickest way to reach this mountian eyrie is by cable car *(June–Sept Mon noon–1pm, Tue–Fri 7.45am–1pm, Sat/Sun 8.45am–2pm, Oct–Easter Mon noon–8.30pm, Tue–Sat 7.45am–8.30pm, Sun 9.30am–midnight (single ticket 3.50, return 6 euros | www.funiviaerice.it)*.

The stylish *Hotel Elimo (21 rooms | tel. 09 23 86 93 77 | www.hotelelimo.it | Expensive)* and INSIDER TIP *Hotel Moderno (40 rooms | tel. 09 23 86 93 00 | www.hotelmodernoerice.it | Moderate)* are in beautiful old town *palazzi*. Very good food can be found in *Monte San Giuliano (closed Mon | tel. 09 23 86 95 95 | Moderate)* including the famous *cuscus alla trapanese*. Less sophisticated, country cooking is to be had in *Ulisse (closed Thu | tel. 09 23 86 93 33 | Budget–Moderate)*, where you can sit in the shady garden. Information: *STR | Via Guarrasi 1 | tel. 09 23 86 93 88*

SAN VITO LO CAPO
(129 D2) *(🕮 C3)*

The 40km (25mi) journey along the jagged coastline is magnificent. Bare rock in *Scurati* with inhabited farmhouses next to deserted houses built in a huge cave. Further inland, the *macchia* becomes more dense, broken up by small fertile fields. This is where a INSIDER TIP trail around the 659m (2162ft) high *Monte Cofano* starts, a completely barren rocky mass that cannot be missed. The circular tour takes approx. 3–4 hours, including a break along the craggy coastline to go for a swim with wonderful views of the shore, the islands and the Zingaro mountain range.

San Vito, that lies in a shallow sandy bay close to the promontory with the lighthouse, has grown up around a mighty Saracen tower that has since been converted into a church. The exposed site, the sandy beach and the bizarre cliff formations of *Torre dell'Impiso* have made this into a popular tourist resort.

Hotel Egitarso (22 rooms | tel. 09 23 97 21 11 | www.hotelegitarso.it | Moderate) is right on the shore and the B&B *Ai Dammusi (2 rooms | tel. 09 23 62 14 94 | www.aidammusisanvito.it | Moderate–Expensive)*, an oriental cube with a domed roof, is on the sandy beach. Information: *town hall | tel. 09 23 97 24 64*

San Vito is well known for its couscous with fish and seafood and a couscous festival is held every year in September. In the other 50 weeks of the year, you can find this speciality in *Alfredo* on the outskirts of the town where the spaghetti with fresh prawns can also be recommended *(Contrada Valanga 3 | tel. 09 23 97 23 66 | Moderate)*, and in *Pocho* in Makari, 5km (3mi) to the south, where the philosopher Marilù Terrasi runs a small 12-roomed hotel and organises musical and theatrical events *(tel. 09 23 97 25 25 | www.pocho.it | Moderate)*.

SCOPELLO ☼ (129 D2) *(🕮 D3)*

Scopello, 35km (22mi) from Trapani, is little more than a fortified farming hamlet located above the cliffs and surrounded by a wall with barren *macchia* beyond. The sea thrashes onto tiny pebbly bays below that are dominated by the *faraglioni* – the high rugged cliffs. To the north is the boundary of *Zingaro* nature reserve. The old shepherds' cottages are now lived in by local craftsmen or are small country guesthouses, some serving traditional home fare: *La Tavernetta (7 rooms | tel. 09 24 54 11 29 | Moderate)* and the converted farmhouse set in a garden next door,

Casa Vito Mazzara (tel. 09 24 54 11 35 | Budget), with seven rooms and 10 flats. You can book a wonderful farm holiday run by *Camillo Finazzo* on a mountain in ✲ *Castello di Baida* with a superb view of the coast *(11 rooms/flats | tel. 0 92 43 80 51 | www.camillofinazzo.com | Budget)*.

A road leads to the INSIDER TIP *Riserva dello Zingaro* (129 D2) *(ⅅ C–D3)*, although the actual nature reserve itself can only be accessed on foot. Don't forget your swimming things as there are any number of little paths down to romantic bays. Fan palms grow in this area in the thousands. Although they are generally low-growing bushes, they can reach a height of 4–5m (13–16ft). You are not allowed to leave the well-tended paths. A 7km (4½mi) long path along the coast is signposted and easy walking, but remember to take lots of water, something to eat and sunscreen. *(Information at both entrances, in Scopello and Torre dell' Uzzo | www.riservazingaro.it | entrance fee incl. hiking map 3 euros)*. Plan approx. 4 hours for the coastal path, there and back; for the circular path half way up and then back along the coast you'll need 5–6 hours.

Ristorante del Golfo in the centre *(closed Tue | Via Segesta 153 | tel. 0 92 43 02 57 | Budget–Moderate)* serves wonderfully and imaginatively prepared fresh seafood caught locally. ✲ Hotel *Al Madarig* (38 rooms | Piazza Petrolo 7 | tel. 0 92 43 35 33 | www.almadarig.com | Moderate) is situated above Castellammare's labyrinthine Old Town with a view of Zingaro's coastline.

SEGESTA ★ ✲ (129 D3) *(ⅅ D4)*

41km (25½mi) southeast of Trapani, in a solitary location in the mountains, are the remains of the amphitheatre and temple of an Elymian town, whose residents had adopted the Greek culture and lifestyle, that has long since disappeared. The 5th-century *colonnaded temple* was never actually completed. The *amphitheatre* slightly further up opens up to the distant sea and the valley below Alcamo. *Daily 9am–6pm | entrance fee 9 euros*

On the *Fiume Caldo* below Segesta there are thermal springs with a high sulphur content that surface at the end of a deep gorge. On the Castellammare road take the turning to ● *Terme Segestane (thermally-heated swimming pool Fri–Wed 9am–1pm and 4.30pm–midnight | entrance fee 7 euros)* after the bridge over the river.

The impressive Doric temple in Segesta

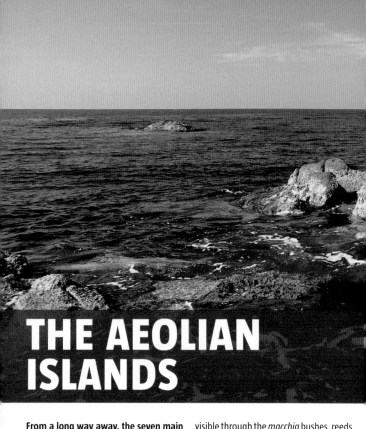

THE AEOLIAN ISLANDS

From a long way away, the seven main islands look like silvery-grey cones hovering above the water. As you draw closer, their volcanic origin becomes perfectly obvious.

The Aeolian (or Lipari) Islands are part of the archipelago around Europe's largest active volcano, the mighty undersea Marsili. Crashing waves have gnawed as the soft tuff and blocks of harder lava can be found along the shoreline which virtually everywhere drops steeply into the sea. Caves, grottoes and arches, small rocky islets and tiny bays and beaches make up a coastline that still remains unspoilt to this day. The colours of the earth and rock are visible through the *macchia* bushes, reeds and tufts of grass, ranging from blinding-white pumice to earthy shades and brilliant reds, greens and jet black lava.

The islands were first settled 6000 years ago. Lipari had the largest deposits of obsidian, the shiny black volcanic glass that was used to make sharp blades, arrowheads, representative daggers and axes up until the Bronze Age. Obsidian from Lipari was exported as far north as Scandinavia, southern Russia and Egypt. Around 1270 BC, the rich deposits drew conquerors from the mainland and it was their king, Liparos, who gave the islands their name. The locals, however, called them 'Isole

Photo: The rugged coastline of Salina

A magical volcanic kingdom: explore a world of caves and grottoes, cliffs, hot springs and secret bays

Eolie', after Aeolus, the ruler of the winds in Greek mythology who dwelt in this corner of the Mediterranean and lashed the islands – as he continues to do today. It is not seldom that storms cut the islands off from the rest of the world for days on end. Lipari, in particular, is a paradise for hikers, Vulcano for hot water fans, Salina is the green island with wonderful wines, Panarea is where celebreties and their entourage

meet, Stromboli's attraction is its fiery volcano, Filicudi and Alicudi are lonely places. The islands have been a Unesco World Heritage Site since 1999.

Ferries, hydrofoils *(aliscafi)* and catamarans operate between Milazzo and Lipari, the central point for reaching all of the other islands, several times a day.

'La cucina eoliana', the islanders' fare, was the art of an extremely poor people scrap-

Fishermen on the quayside in Lipari

ing a living from farming and fishing who nevertheless wanted to gain some enjoyment from their food. Even today, the food they cook makes careful use of what the sea and the gardens provide. The sun, the salty wind off the sea and the minerals in the volcanic earth give tomatoes, aubergines, courgettes and greens an especially intensive aroma. This is accentuated by wild fennel, oregano and capers that no dish goes without and which grow in abundance in every corner of the islands, even in the most barren. In June, you can **INSIDER TIP** pick your own capers along with the islanders. The bushes with their lovely flowers grow all over the place on rocks and walls, particularly on Salina. The buds are mixed with unrefined sea salt which removes the bitter taste and conserves them.

LIPARI

(132 C2) (*Ø K2*) **The town (pop. 4500) with its Baroque façades and capped towers is dwarfed by the massive rock of the acropolis (citadel) with its fortress built in the Middle Ages.**

The houses nestle around the two bays, the *Marina Lunga* where the ferries come in, and the *Marina Corta*, the lively hydrofoil terminal. Behind the Marina Corta with its little chapel island in front and the bars and restaurants around the *piazza*, narrow alleyways lead up to the citadel and into the Old Town. These are followed by the new straight network of roads with houses and gardens, the majority of the hotels and the main thoroughfare, the *Via Vittorio Emanuele.*

The town is surrounded by hills with terraced fields created at considerable effort, which – both here and on the other side of the island – are gradually being abandoned. The farmhouses are white cubes with flat domed roofs which collect rainwater for the cisterns and are used for drying grain, figs and nuts in the summer. The fronts have verandas supported by round pillars made of lava or concrete with a reed roof or a pergola.

THE AEOLIAN ISLANDS

SIGHTSEEING

ACROPOLIS ☀️
The appearance of the citadel, the upper town with churches and noblemen's houses, dates from the Baroque period. Located above the rugged cliffs, this knoll had previously been used by the locals as a place of refuge. The solid medieval town wall had just one gate leading to the Old Town. Today, the pedestrianised acropolis area also has a museum. Reconstructed early tombs and defensive walls can be seen between the churches.

NATIONAL MUSEUM ⭐
In Antiquity and early history, the Aeolian Islands were a central point for trading throughout the Mediterranean. Rich finds from this time, such as stone tools, ceramics and grave artefacts, are exhibited on the acropolis. There is also a department on volcanology. *Mon–Sat 9am–1pm and 3pm–6pm, Sun 9am–1pm | entrance fee 6 euros*

FOOD & DRINK

INSIDER TIP E'PULERA
Aeolian island house in a beautiful garden with jasmin. Local food and creative variations of traditional Sicilian fish dishes are served at stone tables. *May–Oct daily, evenings only | Via Diana 51 | tel. 09 09 81 11 58 | Moderate*

FILIPPINO ●
Excellent island cooking, on the square below the acropolis. *Closed Mon | Piazza Municipio | tel. 09 09 81 10 02 | Moderate*

LE MACINE ☀️
This island house in a garden on the plateau in the village of *Pianoconte* has a fantastic view and good seafood. *Daily | tel. 09 09 82 23 87 | Budget–Moderate*

SHOPPING

Via Vittorio Emanuele is both the place to go for a stroll and to shop. Pretty clothing and some nice bits and bobs can be picked up here.

BEACHES & SPORTS

Boats to the neighbouring islands, beaches and bays depart from the Marina Corta. *Da Massimo (Via Maurolico 2 | tel. 09 09 81 30 86 | www.damassimo.it)* offers boat tours and has rubber boats for hire. *Charter Pesca* on the Marina Grande *(Via Criispi 55 | tel. 09 09 81 49 39 | www.charterpesca eolie.it)* offers fishing trips.

Small cars, scooters and boats can be rented from *Roberto Foti (Via Filippo Mancuso | tel. 09 09 81 13 70 | www.robertofoti.it)*. Those fascinated by the depths of the sea should contact the diving school *La Gorgonia (Salita San Giuseppe | tel. 09 09 81 26 16 | www.la gorgoniadiving.it)*

⭐ **National Museum**
A history and geology tour in Lipari → p. 89

⭐ **Stromboli**
Spectacular: the island's 924m-high active volcano → p. 92

⭐ **Punta Milazzese**
A prehistoric village perches on the southernmost point of Panarea → p. 94

⭐ **Vulcano**
Smoking craters and a wallow in sulphur-smelling hot water → p. 95

MARCO POLO HIGHLIGHTS

Rurally situated island home in a garden above the town. The guesthouse is clean and friendly. *9 rooms | Via Marconi 43 | tel. 09 09 88 01 14 | Moderate–Expensive*

ORIENTE

The 100-year-old villa stands in a garden with a sun terrace just a 5-minute walk from the centre. *32 rooms | Via G. Marconi 35 | tel. 09 09 81 14 93 | www.hoteloriente lipari.com | Moderate*

Information for all the islands available from *STR: Via Vittorio Emanuele 202 | tel. 09 09 88 00 95 | www.aasteolie.191.it* For more information, see the links under *www.eoliearcipelago.it*

TOUR OF THE ISLAND (132 C2) *(𝄐 K2)*
The island can be explored by taking the 33km (20mi) circular tour. The only beaches accessible by land are on the east coast; the west is much more rugged.

Canneto is a long-drawn out fishing village with a rubble beach. Leisurely everyday life takes place along the beach and in the two rows of low houses that line the two parallel roads. The old lava flow, the Forgia Vecchia – where obsidian was once mined – rises up steeply immediately behind. A footpath in front of the now disused pumice quarry leads to *Spiaggia Bianca*, Lipari's most popular beach. Beyond Acquacalda, the road climbs up to the plateau and the farming communities of ⊗ *Quattropani* and *Pianoconte*, which are well worth seeing and from where *Monte Sant'Angelo* (594m/1950ft) and the abandoned spa *Terme di San Calogero* can be reached. From the ⊗ *belvedere* you have a wonderful view of the neigh-

Looking over prickly pear cacti and gorse from Lipari to Vulcano

MARINA CORTA

The area next to the hydrofoil terminal is basically a huge open-air bar where the locals in particular meet.

CASA GIALLA

Holiday on an *agriturismo* tomato and vegetable farm in *Pianoconte* with terraces and verandahs outside the 8 rooms. *Tel. 09 09 81 70 17 | www.casagialla.it | Budget–Moderate*

bouring island, Vulcano. For those on foot, there are tracks and paths down to Lipari past the village *San Bartolo al Monte*, whose pretty church stands at the beginning of the path. A steep footpath into *Valle Muria* branchs off this and leads to a narrow pebbly beach INSIDERTIP *Spiaggia Muria*, where fishing huts have been built into the rock face. A waymarked path to the observatory and the southern-most point of the island starts at the church of San Bartolo, and then climbs up high above the east coast.

SALINA

(132 B–C2) *(J2)* **The three islands to the west are away from the general stream of tourists. Salina is also known as the 'green island' due to is its extensive farming, chiefly producing Malvasia, a sweet white wine, and capers.**

FOOD & DRINK

A' CANNATA
At the beach in *Lingua*, whose lighthouse marks the southeastern point of the island, seafood is served on long tables in the *pineta*. Also has 8 simple rooms and 9 flats. *Daily | tel. 09 09 84 31 61 | www.acannata.it | Moderate*

BEACHES & SPORTS

FOSSA DELLE FELCI
(132 B–C2) *(J2)*
The easily recognisable and partly waymarked trail starts at the harbour *Santa Marina Salina* and zig-zags its way up the long-since extinct volcano to the top at 962m (3156ft), the highest peak in the Aeolian Islands with an extensive panorama. From here, you can go down to Leni and Rinella. It was in INSIDERTIP *Pollara*,

which consists of just a few cuboid houses, and in the fishermen's dwellings carved out of the caves in the cliffs on the tiny beach, that Michael Radford directed the award-winning film *Il Postino* (The Postman), starring Philippe Noiret as Pablo Neruda, in 1994. Pebbly beaches to the east, otherwise almost exclusively a rocky coastline with cliffs that is only accessible from land in a few places *(Punta di Scario* near *Malfa, Pollara* and *Rinella)*.

WHERE TO STAY

HOTEL ARIANA
Art Nouveau villa in *Rinella* on the south coast, with a terrace above the sea. Restaurant. *15 rooms | tel. 09 09 80 90 75 | www.hotelariana.it | Expensive*

HOTEL SIGNUM
The large villa in the centre of *Malfa* has been turned into a 4-star hotel; good

LOW BUDGET

▶ Take the ferry rather than the hydrofoil or catamaran. The crossing takes twice as long but costs less than half the price.

▶ The *Baia Unci* campsite on Canneto beach on Lipari has 8 reasonably-priced bungalows and 10 flats as well as spaces for tents. *Via Marina Garibaldi | tel. 09 09 811 9 09 | www.campingbaiaunci.it*

▶ *Camere Diana Brown:* pleasant accommodation in a side road off the central Corso Vittorio Emanuele in Lipari. *12 rooms | tel. 09 09 81 25 84 or 33 86 40 75 72 | www.dianabrown.it*

cuisine. *30 rooms | tel. 09 09 84 42 22 | www.hotelsignum.it | Expensive*

WHERE TO GO

The population of Alicudi and Filicudi, the two islands to the west, has sunk more dramatically than on neighbouring islands. Sheep and goat farming, wine production and cereal crops are no longer viable; as tourist destinations they may well be pretty, but their distance from the other islands makes day-trips that much more difficult.

ALICUDI (132 A2) *(Ⓜ H2)* ●
The island, a perfectly formed volcanic cone rising out of the sea, is an oasis for those looking for utter peace and quiet. There are only 105 people still living here. Accommodation and food is available in private houses or in the one hotel on the island. The houses – the majority of which have been abandoned – have been built in terraced fields along the main route that leads from the harbour up to the peak at a height of 675m. *Hotel Ericusa*, with 12 simple rooms, is just a few yards from the harbour; the restaurant always serves fresh fish *(May–Sept | tel. 09 09 88 99 02 | www.alicudihotel.it | Moderate)*. Approx. 70 min. from Salina by catamaran

FILICUDI (132 A–B2) *(Ⓜ J2)*
The island is dry and covered in high grass and reed. A long scree beach starts at the harbour *Filicudi Porto* and extends as far as the cliffs at Capo Graziano, where the walls of a prehistoric settlement of circular huts can be found on the knoll. A road leads across the plateau past fields and clusters of houses to the main settlement on the island, *Pecorini*, and down to the harbour and beach at Pecorini Mare. The majority of the coastline with its grottoes, cliffs and rocky pinacles can only be accessed by boat. The restaurant *Villa La Rosa* has three pretty guest bedrooms, and the food conjured up by Signora Adelaide is among the best on the island. Apart from seafood, she serves rabbit and bakes her own bread *(Via Rosa | Rocca Ciauli | Filicudi | tel. 09 09 88 99 65 | www.villalarosa.it | Moderate)*. The hotel *La Canna* in Rocca Ciauli has a lovely location high above Filicudi Porto *(14 rooms | tel. 09 09 88 99 56 | www.lacannahotel.it | Moderate)*. The *Apogon Diving Center* in *Hotel Phenicusa* in Filicudi Porto offers courses, equipment and bottle refills. *(Tel. 09 09 88 99 55 | www.apogon.it)*. Approx. 35 min. from Salina by catamaran

STROMBOLI

(133 D1) *(Ⓜ K–L1)* ⭐ **Set apart to the north of the others, is the island of Stromboli (pop. 350) with its active volcano, over the summit of which there is always a thin plume of smoke.**
The few cuboid houses in *Ginostra* in the south form Italy's most isolated settlement. Buildings straggle the only road towards the north. On every hill is a church, the focal point of the three villages on the island – *San Vincenzo, Ficogrande* and *Piscità*. A paved path through the high reeds, which later turns into an unmade one with a few dangerous spots, starts at the lighthouse and leads up to the summit. Groups of hikers normally set off in the afternoon to reach the top before sunset to enjoy the nocturnal spectacle of sheaves of embers that are catapulted out of the crater at short intervals. Hikers must be accompanied by a mountain guide and helmets are compulsory. Take torches and a set of new batteries with you and wear warm, windproof clothing! **INSIDER TIP** *Virtual walks* on the Internet: *www.swisseduc.ch/stromboli/volcano/virtual*

THE AEOLIAN ISLANDS

FOOD & DRINK

LA LAMPARA
Open-air pizzeria with a large terrace and a pizza chef from Naples. *Daily | Via Vittorio Emanuele | Ficogrande | tel. 0 90 98 64 09 | Budget*

PUNTA LENA ● ∿
Exquisite, light, regional cuisine; terrace with pergola and marvellous views. *April–Oct daily | Via Marina 8 | tel. 0 90 98 62 04 | Expensive*

BEACHES & SPORTS

A long scree and gravel beach with black sand in places stretches the length of the three villages on the north coast.

MAGMATREK
Cooperative of volcano guides (also English-speaking). *Via Vittorio Emanuele | tel. 09 09 86 57 68 | www.magmatrek.it.* Appropriate clothing available in the sports

shop *Totem (Piazza S. Vincenzo | tel. 09 09 86 57 52)*, also for hire.

WHERE TO STAY

Accommodation is expensive. Landladies with private rooms to rent meet boats when they come in. Basic accommodation costs 25 euros p.p. in the low season.

FRANCESCO AQUILONE
Small, friendly guesthouse in San Vincenzo, in luxuriant garden with lemon trees, fisherman's fare. *5 rooms | Via Vittorio Emanuele 29 | tel. 0 90 98 60 80 | www. aquiloneresidence.it | Budget–Moderate*

LA SIRENETTA PARK HOTEL
In 1950, Ingrid Bergman and the crew in Roberto Rossellini's film 'Stromboli' stayed here, in what was then a very modest inn. Today, the hotel on the beach in Ficogrande has 55 comfortable rooms. *April–Oct | tel. 0 90 98 60 25 | www.lasirenetta.it | Expensive*

An eerily beautiful spectacle at night: lava pours down the flanks of Stromboli

PANAREA (132 C2) (*ω K1*)

Panarea is the smallest and most fashionable of the islands – in summer, celebreties and their hangers-on rub shoulders here with those from the worlds of commerce and banking. The island is surrounded by numerous rocky outcrops and islets that stick out of the sea – the remains of a collapsed volcano. The three villages *Ditella*, *San Pietro* with its harbour, and *Drauto* run into one another, scattered picturesquely up the jet-black rocky slopes. The west coast is inaccessible, whereas a path down the east coast links the hot steaming fumaroles in the north with ⭐ *Punta Milazzese* in the south where, on a ledge 20m above the sea, the walls of a prehistoric village of circular huts can be seen. A path leads to the dreamlike bay *Cala Junco* surrounded by cliffs. The little island offshore and the rocky cove are the perfect place for swimming and snorkelling. Experience the expertise at creating exquisite dishes with simple ingredients at *Da Pina* with its verandah and garden (*7 rooms | Via San Pietro 3 | tel. 0 90 98 30 32 | www.dapina.com | Expensive*). *Hycesia*, with good seafood, is intimate and – for Panarea – reasonably priced (*March–Oct | tel. 0 90 98 30 41 | www.*

BOOKS & FILMS

▶ **Inspector Montalbano** – is a Sicilian through and through. He loves good honest food and is always chasing women. The cases were largely filmed in Porto Empedocle and Agrigento, where the author Andrea Camilleri grew up. The detective novels and television series depict everyday crimes on the island.

▶ **The Leopard** – The partly autobiographical novel by Giuseppe Tomasi di Lampedusa focuses on the lives of the aristocracy at the time of Italian Unification. Luchino Visconti's marvellously evocative film of 1963, starring Burt Lancaster and Alain Delon, was filmed in many of the original locations.

▶ **Cinema Paradiso** – The setting of the cult film (1988) by Giuseppe Tornatore starring Philippe Noiret is in the mountain eyries of Castelbuono and Palazzo Adriano: a declaration of love for the cinema.

▶ **Stromboli** – The Italian-American film (1950) was directed by Roberto Rossellini and starred Ingrid Bergman. It features documentary-like scenes of the fishermen's life and an actual evacuation after an eruption of the volcano. As most villagers are played by actual people from the island, it paints a realistic picture of how the islanders lived.

▶ **Cosa Nostra: A History of the Sicilian Mafia** – John Dickie's account (published in 2004) of the sinister, horrific reality of how the Mafia gained its hold and has maintained its powerful position to this day, infiltrating all levels of society and politics, makes a chilling read.

▶ **Reversible Destiny** – by Peter T. and Jane C. Schneider (2003), based on extensive research in Palermo, also traces the history of the Sicilian mafia.

hycesia.it | *Moderate* | *8 rooms Moderate–Expensive*). The *Raya*, a hotel with terraced gardens, is built in the local venacular. Although it only has 2 stars, its simplicity acts like a magnet for the wealthy. With a boutique and open-air disco *(April–Oct | 29 rooms | tel. 0 90 98 30 13 | www.hotel raya.it | Expensive*). *30–35 minutes from Stromboli by catamaran*

VULCANO

(132 C3) *(⌕ K2)* ⭐ **This island (pop. 450), owes its popularity as a bathing holiday destination to its two bays and their beaches, *Porto Levante* and *Porto Ponente*, where there are cliffs, sand and hot fumaroles that don't just heat the water in a few select spots, but with the hot-water and mud-bath *Acqua del Bagno* provide a freely accessible spa area.**

A waymarked path leads up to the main crater, the *Gran Cratere*. The smell of pungent sulphur may well indicate that the volcano is dormant but it is still very much alive deep down inside and could well erupt again. A 🚶 road along an elevated plain with paroramic views leads to the centre of the island, to *Piano*. A tiny road with hairpin bends carries on to 🚶 *Gelso lighthouse* right in the south, which has a magnificent view of the north coast of Sicily and the wall-like Nebrodi mountains behind it, with the summit of Mount Etna towering above them in the far distance.

Not pretty but healthy: wallowing in the mud on Vulcano

FOOD & DRINK

MARIA TINDARA
High up on the mountain in Piano, very traditional, serving rabbit, lamb and homemade pasta. *Daily | tel. 09 09 85 30 04 | Moderate*

DA MAURIZIO
Serving imaginative seafood dishes. Near the harbour. *Daily | tel. 09 09 84 24 26 | Moderate*

WHERE TO STAY

GARDEN VULCANO
This former captain's house has an impressive collection of memorabilia from around the world. Hotel guests also benefit from free entrance to the thermal pool in the Terme di Vulcano. *37 rooms | Porto Ponente | tel. 09 09 85 21 06 | www.hotelgardenvulcano.it | Moderate–Expensive*

ROJAS BAHIA
The hotel is surrounded by a wide green space near the beach in Porto Levante. *28 rooms | April–Sept | tel. 09 09 85 20 80 | www.hotelrojas.com | Moderate–Expensive*

TRIPS & TOURS

The tours are marked in green in the road atlas, pull-out map and on the back cover

1

TRACKING DOWN THE WHITE GOLD ON THE VIA DEL SALE

The Via del Sale, the Salt Route, runs along minor roads down the coast from Trapani to Marsala. As clear as the boundary between the sea and the land may appear to be where the low-lying limestone meets the water, optically the sky, the salt-pits, the lagoons and the flat islands with their rows of pine trees and deserted houses merge into one: a melancholic landscape. The cragged rocky peak of Eryx looms up above the plains just as suddenly as the three islands Favignana, Levanzo and Marettimo appear out of the water. The route is only 55km (34mi) long and as flat as a pancake – and therefore ideal for cyclists – but to have enough time to visit the island of Mozia, you should plan a whole day and have a picnic en route. The long, hot summer and the virtually incessant breeze favour the industry that has prospered here in harmony with its natural surroundings for hundreds of years, producing salt with the help of water, the sun, wind and human labour. From 1960 onwards, one salt-pit after another was shut down and the windmills fell into disrepair. In 1984, when the salt

Photo: Traditional salt production in the salt-pans near Trapani

Wheat and wine, salt and sulphur: exploring the lesser-known Sicily away from main roads

lakes were earmarked for oil refineries, conservationists started to fight to retain this unique landscape and to get some of the salt-pans and their windmills working once again. Today, about half of the area previously worked is now operating. Two sites have museums and five windmills have been restored. These mills drive the pumps for the salt water as well as the millstones that grind the blocks of salt.

In Trapani → p. 81 take the minor road to Marsala (signposted Airport/Birgi, later Via del Sale). 5km (3mi) south of Trapani there is a turning to the Salina di Nubia. The different stages of salt production are shown in the Museo del Sale (*daily 9.30am–1.30pm and 3.30pm–6.30pm | entrance fee 2 euros*). Returning to the minor road, head for Marsala until you reach the turning to Birgi Novo, a village of single-storey houses surrounded by vineyards, beyond the airport. Carry along this narrow lane to the south, always keeping to the banks of the lagoon. Between 30cm and 4m (1–13ft) deep, it attracts lots of water birds and has a wealth of underwater flora. On a level with the island of Mozia is the largest operating salt-pan, INSIDER TIP *Ettore Infersa (daily 9am–8pm | entrance fee 5 euros | www. salineettoreinfersa.com)*. You can visit the salt lakes, a museum and a windmill and buy some of the white gold too. There are also 3 rooms with a view of the salt works for overnight guests *(Moderate)*. Boats to Mozia leave from here *(9am–2 hours before sunset | 6 euros)*.

Mozia ★ has a profusion of pines, palms and vineyards. The island was a fortified Phoenician port until its destruction by the Greeks in 397 BC. Impressive ruins still exist today. A walk around the whole island takes between 2 and 3 hours. In the south are the basins and walls of the 2500-year-old harbour; in the north an urn graveyard with roughly-hewn gravestones, the *tophet*, and the Cappiddazzu excavation site, a monumental temple to Tanit, the principal goddess together with Baal, of the Carthaginians who turned the island into a strategic base. The villa once belonging to the English wine magnet Joseph Whitaker now houses a museum with finds from the Punic past of Mozia and Marsala. The highlight is a life-sized marble figure, the *Ephebe of Mozia*, a Greek sculpture from the 5th century BC of a young male figure dressed in a robe with a wealth of folds. *(Museum and archaeological area daily 9am–3pm, March–Sept until 7pm | entrance fee 9 euros)*. Retuning from the island of Mozia, the road to Marsala → p. 77 keeps to the coast, passing through fishing villages and past holiday homes.

The now not-so-youthful
Ephebe of Mozia

2 FIELDS OF WHEAT AND SULPHUR MINES

🚗 The region around Caltanissetta was an industrial area from 1720 until 1920. Around 80% of the world's sulphur – an indispensable raw material for gunpowder and the chemical industry – was mined here. Today, the endless ranges of hills and mountains have been returned to crops as it used to be in Antiquity when central Sicily was the Romans' granary. This route, for which you should plan at least one day, will take you 200km (124mi) from Enna – Sicily's 'navel' – to Agrigento via Caltanissetta, mostly along little-used minor roads.

Road 121 leads from Enna → p. 49 into the wide valley of the *Fiume Salso*. The *autostrada* twists through the countryside here sometimes on bridges that are up to 10km (6mi) long. In Villarosa, there are INSIDER TIP seven, bright-red goods wagons at the station which the former stationmaster has turned into a museum on the history of the area and the railway, sulphur mining, agriculture and emigration. To date, there are 2500 objects ranging from a whistle to a prince's bedroom, collected from Villarossa, the rest of Sicily and from all over the world *(Tue–Sun 9.30am–noon, 4.30pm–7.30pm | entrance fee 3.50 euros | www.trenomuseovillarosa. it)*. Good, hearty food can be found in the trattoria La Littorina, also housed in a railway carriage *(closed Mon | tel. 32 05 66 55 24 | Budget)*.

The market stands, street kitchens and narrow alleyways in the Old Town of the former mining centre Caltanissetta are a bit like an oriental bazaar. For something different try Vicolo Duomo *(closed Mon | Vicolo Niviera 1 | Budget)* in the Old Town. Hotel Plaza *(32 rooms | Via Gaetani 5 | tel. 09 34 58 38 77 | www.hotelplazacaltanis setta.it | Moderate)*, also in the Old Town, can be recommended as a place to stay. Mussomeli is reached via San Cataldo. 2km (1¼mi) before you get there you will pass ✂️ Castello Manfredonico from the 12th century located on a rocky promontory that made it unassailable. From the top, you can see most of Sicily on a clear day.

Casteltermini and San Biagio are small towns at the foot of Monti Sicani, with its forests and many springs. It is worth making a short detour to the pilgrim church of Santa Rosalia di Quisquina where the patron saint of Palermo lived in a cave as a hermit in the 12th century. ✂️ Monte Cammarata which rises up to 1578m (5177ft) provides a lovely view as far as Etna and across the sea.

From here, the route continues to San Angelo Muxaro, a small town boldly sited on a mountain plateau. Below the town is a waymarked footpath from the road to prehistoric rock tombs. The **INSIDER TIP** *Vulcanelli di Macalube* are reached from

Gently undulating hilly countryside near Enna

Aragona, approx. 15km (9½mi) further on. These are mud craters in which bubbles form, caused by gas forced up from deep down in the earth. In Antiquity they were considered one of the entrances to the Underworld or as cursed places. Information is available and tours can be booked in the Riserva Naturale Macalube *(Aragona | Via Salvatore La Rosa | tel. 09 22 69 92 10)*. From Aragona, the shortest route to Agrigento → p. 72 is 15km (9½mi). However, a much more interesting route – albeit 40km (25mi) longer – takes you to the two Baroque country towns Favara and Naro. Here, sculptors and stonemasons let their fantasy run

Mussomeli: Castello Manfredonico

wild and carved faces, masks, grotesque caryatids, pillars, sills and squiggles out of the soft, dark-yellow sandstone to adorn the façades of churches and palaces. Build up your strength again in the village trattoria **Cacciatore** in nearby **Castrofilippo** *(Via Verdi 5 | tel. 09 22 82 98 24 | closed Wed | Budget)*.

3 THE GREEN GIANTS OF PIANO POMO

The Madonie Mountains are the central part of a long chain that rises above Sicily's north coast. Inland, they form an upland plateau that is between 1500m (5000ft) and almost 2000m (6600ft) high. It is partly covered by forest although most is grass steppe with a few individual giant trees. The giant holly trees of Piano Pomo are the oldest of their kind in Europe. The hike takes about 2½ hours. Hiking boots are recommended. And don't forget to take lots of water with you.

The start of this mountain hike is Piano Sempria (1260m/4134ft), which you can reach from Castelbuono along a 10km (6mi) long mountain road. Rooms and hearty food, such as tagliatelle with mushrooms and pork from 'free-range pigs', are to be had at the mountain lodge ☺ Rifugio Francesco Crispi *(28 beds | tel. 09 21 67 22 79 | www.ristorantiitaliani.it/rifugio francescocrispi | Budget)*.

An information board at the beginning of the path shows the route. At the hollow, 800-year-old oak, in which there is a small statue of the Virgin Mary, the path crosses the road and zig-zags its way up through the steep oak woodland to a ☀ view point.

The climb finishes here and the path continues below a rock face along the slope and runs into a track which passes over a cattle grid onto the grassy Piano Pomo

plain (1380m/4528ft). There is a *pagliaro* here – an elogated stone building with a roof of brushwood, with tables and benches inside. It has been built for forest workers and hikers along the lines of a Sicilian shepherd's hut.

Climb over the fence using the wooden steps and after a few yards down a path you'll come to a grove of giant holly trees that has its origins in the Ice Age. There are around 100 trees that reach a height of up to 15m (50ft) and are estimated to be 300 years old and more. It is quite dark among the thick trunks as little light penetrates the dense foliage. Beyond the grove, an easily recognisable path leads through beech and oak woodland, with equally huge treetrunks, to the ☀ cross on the summit of Cozzo Luminario (1512m/4961ft), from which you have a panoramic view in all directions taking in the sea, the Aeolian Islands, Etna and the high plateau of Pizzo Carbonara (1979m/6493ft). The path then descends into a dip in the karst rocks and onto a forest track that will bring you back to Piano Sempria. More information is available under *www. parcodellemadonie.it/sentiero-degli-agri fogli-giganti.html*

4 SICILY'S NORTHERN POINT AROUND MESSINA

This tour goes from Messina to the northernmost point on the island and then up to the ridge of the Monti Peloritani (with views of the straits, the coast and the mountains of Calabria, the Aeolian Islands, the Ionian and Tyrrhenian Seas), then on to Monte Dinnamare and back to Messina. Choose a clear day and take a picnic with you before you set off on your mountainbike or by car.

The first 25km (15½mi) of the 65km (40mi) circular tour follow the coast along the increasingly narrow strait to Sicily's northern point called ☼ **Punta del Faro** or **Capo Peloro**. From the beach you can see the Rock of Scilla on the other side of the strait and the whirlpools just off the coast that form in the shallows and along the sandbanks of Cariddi. They pose a danger to small ships even today. In Greek mythology they take the form of the sea monsters Scylla and Charybdis. The fishing village **Ganzirri** lies between the promontory and the two lagoon pools that are famous for mussel farming. You can sample the fish and mussels in the **Trattoria Napoletana** *(closed Wed | tel. 0 90 39 10 32)* with a view across the strait. Between **Punta del Faro** and **Spartà**, Sicily's most northerly point, there are several beaches where you can swim, with cliffs alternating with sandy and pebbly

beaches. The road then runs along the ridge of the Peloritani mountains to **Colle San Rizzo** (624m/2047ft) and along the same road to ☼ **Monte Dinnamare**, 1130m (3707ft) above sea level, where there is a pilgrim church dedicated to the Virgin Mary. The woods in the vicinity with cool springs and picnic places are the ideal spot for a relaxing break. The view from up here takes in the Tyrrhenian Sea and Sicily's north, the Aeolian Islands and, to the east, Messina and Calabria's southern headland. To the south and west you can make out the mountain valleys and peaks in the Peloritani Mountains. Returning to Colle San Rizzo, it is worth making a detour half way back to Messina, to **Badiazza**, the romantic ruins of a fortified church with a tower and battlements from the Norman period.

Ciao Italia: looking across to mainland Italy from the beach at the Punta del Faro

SPORTS & ACTIVITIES

Sicily boasts a coastline of more than 1000km (620mi). With the exception of a few short sections around major urban centres, the water is invitingly clean. Watersports such as snorkelling and diving, sailing and surfing are possible all round the island. On *terra firma*, hikers, mountainbikers and horseriders in particular get their money's worth too.

DIVING

Ideal conditions prevail for divers and snorkellers above rocky terrain. This can be found off the north coast in particular, on the east coast around Etna and the area north of Augusta. By far the best diving grounds are around the small islands – first and foremost Ustica as well as Lampedusa off the coast of Africa. The area around the Aegadian and Aeolian Islands, however, is almost as good.

All islands have a well-established infrastructure for underwater fans (diving courses, equipment for hire, cylinder service, decompression tanks).

Diving around *Ustica* (ferry or hydrofoil from Palermo): the waters are a protected maritime reserve and are considered by Italian divers to be the best of their kind. In summer packed; otherwise sufficient private accommodation available. Infor-

Up mountains, in the countryside, under water and in the air: the best places for your favourite sports and activities

mation: *Riserva Marina di Ustica | tel. 09 18 44 94 56 (tourist office) | www.ustica.net*

GOLF

Two 18-hole courses in exceptionally beautiful settings have been laid out, paying careful attention to the ancient trees on two estates. On the northern flank of Mount Etna, 650m (2100ft) above sea level, is the *Picciolo Golf Club* with its own guesthouse *(Moderate–Expensive)*. The greens are among oak and hazle trees and vines *(Castiglione di Sicilia | tel. 09 42 98 62 52 | www.ilpicciologolf.com)*. *Le Madonie Golf Club (Collesano | tel. 09 21 93 43 87 | www.lemadoniegolf.com)* is situated above the coast between Cefalù and Termini Imerese among orange and olive groves.

HIKING

Up until now, the mountains, wild upland plateaus and impressive gorges, especially those in the south, are largely sought out by local hikers. Many trails follow the *trazzeri*, the old cattle routes, that are no longer used today. There are few maps marking footpaths for hikers and few signposts. However, in the five large nature reserves – Etna, the River Alcantara, the Nebrodi, Madonie and Monti Sicani chains – you will be able to find your way easily and choose between hikes of varying degrees of difficulty. Hiking through gorges, which often carry water at all times of year, is only suitable for experienced mountaineers. Guided hikes in the nature reserves are generally available at the weekends.

Cava d'Ispica: 10km (6¼mi)-long gorge with caves at either end that can be visited. Tours depart from the *Ispica visitor centre* at the entrance to the gorge.

Parco Regionale delle Madonie | Petralia Sottana | Corso Pietro Agliata 16 | tel. 09 21 68 40 11 | www.parcodellemadonie.it

Parco Regionale dei Nebrodi | Alcara Li Fusi | Via Ugo Foscolo 1 | tel. 09 41 79 39 04 | www.parcodeinebrodi.it

Parco Regionale dell'Etna | Nicolosi | tel. 0 95 82 11 11 | www.parcoetna.ct.it

Parco Fluviale dell'Alcantara | Via dei Mulini | Francavilla di Sicilia | tel. 09 42 98 99 11 | www.parcoalcantara.it

Parco Regionale dei Monti Sicani | Palazzo Adriano & Bivona | www.parcodeisicani.it You can take a visual hike on the web under *www.greenstontrek.com* which has photos and tours descriptions for hikes in Peloritani, Nebrodi and around Etna; see also under *www.artemisianet.it*.

MOUNTAINBIKING

Mountainbiking is popular among Sicilians and it is possible to cycle virtually all over the island along little-used roads, tracks across farmland and through forests. Etna, Madonie, Nebrodi and the Peloritani mountains in the northeast have challenging changes in altitude, often rising above 1000m (3000ft). It is less strenuous along the south coast, in the west and on the limestone plains around Syracuse and Ragusa.

A lovely tour leads along the **INSIDER TIP** *ridge of the Peloritani mountains* with views over the northernmost point of Sicily, the strait, the Calabrian mountains and Etna, the Aeolian Islands and the Tyrrhenian and Ionian Seas. The tour starts in *Messina* at the *Portella di Rizzo* (466m/1529ft), running along the ridge (1100–1200m/3600–4000ft) to *Portella Mandrazzi* (1125m/3691ft), then twists through a series of hairpin bends to *Castroreale/Milazzo* or *Taormina* – a total of 95km (59mi) from Messina to Taormina. Good, up-to-date information (in English) under *www.sizilien-rad.de*

PARAGLIDING

INSIDER TIP Paragliding *(parapendio)* in Sicily is possible from the high range of mountains in the north, especially in the Nebrodi Mountains, and above Palermo (Piana degli Albanesi, San Cipirello and Gibilrossa). *Accademia Siciliana Volo Libero | Via degli Astronauti 14 | Altofonte | tel. 09 16 64 05 35 | www.asvl.it*

RIDING

Riding is popular, especially in the Madonie Mountains, either as part of a guided day's ride or over several days. Many *agriturismo* farms offer riding. For riding in the Madonie Mountains try: *Azienda Agrituristica Monaco di Mezzo | Petralia Sottana | tel. 09 34 67 39 49 | www.monacodimezzo.com*

Keeping dry: exploring caves in the Alcantara Gorge the easy way

SAILING

First-class sailing is possible between Tropea (Calabria), the Aeolian Islands and along the north coast from Tindari to Cefalù. Passing through the Strait of Messina, the *Stretto*, is an exciting experience. This is a very demanding stretch of water due to the shallows, changing currents, sudden winds and the traffic, and takes in Etna and the attractive east coast with numerous small fishing ports as far as Catania.

WINDSURFING

The best places to surf are on the west and south coasts as there is almost always sufficient wind: San Vito Lo Capo, Favignana, Torre Granitola and Triscina near Selinunt, Torre di Gaffe near Licata and Capo Passero in the southeast. Capo Orlando on the north coast is also popular among surfers.

WINTER SPORTS

The two winter sports areas on Sicily are Etna and the Madonie Mountains where, concentrated in just a few spots, are hotels, lifts, ski schools and downhill slopes cheek by jowl. At weekends when the weather is good, things are very busy especially from January until March when you can be certain of snow. On the south side of Mount Etna, above Nicolosi, 1800m (5900ft) above sea level, is the main winter sports centre which – despite the recent eruptions – has a number of ski runs and lifts as well as accommodation. In the Madonie Mountains, almost everything is centred on *Piano Battaglia* (1650m/ 5410ft). The tracks high up in the Nebrodi and Madonie mountains are ideal for cross-country skiing. These are partly marked as hiking trails and as the long-distance path *Sentiero Italia*.

TRAVEL WITH KIDS

All Italians are wild about children. They would do anything for *bambini* even when they are not their own. And parents are automatically part and parcel of this open demonstration of kindness, whether on a beach, in a hotel or elsewhere.

Sicily has a number of superb holiday adventures in store for children – much more than just sand, sun and ice cream, even if it may not seem the perfect holiday destination for children at first glance. Museums with their endless corridors and showcases packed with objects, excavation sites stretching over several square miles and exposed to the scorching sun, churches, monasteries and palaces on every corner, virtually all of which are 'must-sees' in their own right, and the relatively long distances along never-ending twisty roads with no shade: all these things are pretty demanding on children.

Apart from the Luna Park with its merry-go-rounds and beaches with bright plastic toys which can be found in most seaside holiday resorts, there is little for children and even less that comes with the stamp: 'educationally beneficial'. But 'when in Rome' ... do as the Sicilians do! Take advantage of the cool mornings, enjoy a siesta with the children and have a qiet afternoon. In the evening it is a bit cooler and you'll feel fitter again.

Photo: Boat trip on the Tyrrhenian Sea with Stromboli in the background

Exceptionally family-friendly: boat trips and railways journeys, exploring caves, puppet theatres and as much sea as you could want

In restaurants in Italy, even five-year-olds are considered 'normal' eaters even if they only jab at the food put in front of them. If your child doesn't want spaghetti or the fish, just let the waiter know. He'll understand and accept it. Go for picnics like the Sicilians do, especially at the weekends, when things get pretty hectic elsewhere. There are masses of picnic sites in the wooded mountains, many with spring wa-

ter fountains which can be used to keep fruit and drinks for the children nice and cool.

Flat beaches with fine, soft sand where children can splash around quite safely, dig or build sandcastles, cannot be found all over Sicily. There is a long sandbank south of Syracuse that runs almost 300km (185mi), virtually the whole length of the south coast as far as Selinunte, with the exception of a few rocky sections. The softest and finest sand is in *Fontane Bianche* near Syracuse and on the *Marina di Noto*; south of Ragusa are the wide beaches and dunes of *Pozzallo, Sampieri, Donnalucata* and *Scoglitti*, near *Falconara* to the west of Gela, in *San Leone* (Agrigento) with a number of beach facilities, around *Siciliana Marina*, in *Eraclea Minoa*, around the mouth of the *Fiume Platani* southeast of Sciacca, *Porto Palo di Menfi* and *Marinella* near Selinunte. In the north and east there are only a few short sections, but the water here can get deep quite suddenly. The best places include *San Vito Lo Capo* (town beach), *Mondello* near Palermo with unpolluted water and flour-like sand, *Cefalù* (town beach), *Capo Orlando*, the coast between Tindari and Milazzo, *Letoianni, Giardini-Naxos* with the extremely child-friendly but often overcrowded beaches of *San Marco* and *Fondachello* to the south, and finally the flat plain south of Catania with a number of lidos and beach communities. The islands around Sicily have very few beaches suitable for children.

THE NORTHEAST

GOLA ALCANTARA (133 D5) *(ﾛ K4)*
Wade through the river in the gorge which includes pools for swimming and little whirlpools, either barefooted or in wellies. The latter can be hired. Steps and lift to the river. *On the Taormina–Randazzo road*

THE SOUTHEAST

INSIDER TIP▶ BUSCEMI – REDISCOVERING OLD TRADES (135 D4) *(ﾛ K7)*
A tour of this village, where traditional trades have been given a new lease of life, is a mixture of a visit to a museum and to craft workshops. Look into the various buildings and watch basket-makers and weavers working. *Museo della Civiltà*

Contadina | Mon–Fri 9am–1.30pm and 3pm–6pm, Sat/Sun 9am–1pm | tel. 09 31 87 85 28 | guided tour (2 hrs.) 5 euros, children up to 6 free, 6–18 years old 2.50 euros | www.museobuscemi.org

RAILWAY TRIP
(134–135 B5–E4) *(ﾛ J–K7)*
Between Syracuse and Vittoria, a regular train service climbs up to the high plateau of Ragusa from sea level and back down to the sea again in a 3–4 hour journey which is better than any museum line. It twists and turns around massive bends and loops, crosses several deep gorges, sometimes on heart-stoppingly high viaducts. *3 × daily | fare 8.60 euros, children upto 12 years old 4.30 euros*

THE DONKEYS OF ROSOLINI
(135 D5) *(ﾛ K8)*
Oasi degli Asini is a non-profit organisation that looks after and trains donkey. Your children can go for a donkey ride or even go on little excursions. Accompanied day tours and excurions over a longer period are also available. These will take you through gorges and across the high plateaus of Monti Iblei. You sleep either in tents or on farms and the cooking is done outside. A visit to the *Oasi* includes farmhouses, a playground, volleyball and *boccia* grounds, and a picnic site with barbeque area. *Rosolini | Contrada Santa Croce | tel. 09 31 50 21 79 and 36 87 83 11 76 | www. oasidegliasini.it*

THE NORTH COAST

INSIDER TIP▶ CAVE DWELLINGS AND SPERLINGA CASTLE (131 F3) *(ﾛ H4)*
Some of the caverns under this castle near Nicosia are still lived in today, others are stables and some are readily accessible. There are guided tours of the castle which has a museum on the cave dwellings.

Daily 9.30am–1.30pm, 2.30pm–6.30pm | tel. 09 35 64 30 25 | entrance fee 2 euros, children 1 euro

FIUMARA D'ARTE MAZE
(131 E2) (𝄞 H4)

This modern maze is on a promontory near Castel di Lucio/Castel di Tusa. Finding your way to the middle and out again is not difficult. *Information: Hotel Atelier sul Mare | Castel di Tusa | free entrance | tel. 09 21 33 42 95 | www.ateliersulmare.it*

MARIONETTE THEATRE
IN MONREALE ● (130 B1) (𝄞 E3)

Munna | Cortile Manin 15 | tel. 09 16 40 45 42 and *Sanicola | Via Torres 1 | tel. 09 16 40 94 41*

MARIONETTE THEATRE IN PALERMO ●
(130 B1) (𝄞 E3)

Mimmo Cuticchio | Via Bara 52 | tel. 0 91 32 34 00; Teatro Ippogrifo | Vicolo Ragusi 4 | tel. 0 91 32 91 94 and the theatre in the *Museo Internazionale delle Marionette | Piazzetta Niscemi 5 | tel. 0 91 32 80 60*

Apart form epics, Sicilian tales of knights of old are performed in marionette theatres *(opera* or *teatri dei pupi)*. These include Charlemagne's struggle against the Saracens or the wooing of the beautiful Geneviève which always involve a lot of action and the clinking of swords.

THE TRAPANI SALT WORKS
(128 C3) (𝄞 C4)

In the middle of the salt-pans near Trapani there is an old windmill that has been converted into a museum. Visitors can see how the salt water was pumped from one evaporation basin to the next in the days before electricity was invented, and how the boulders of crystallised salt are ground. Canoes are available for hire. There are boat trips around Mozia lagoon and to the islands in the shallow sea *Stagno di Marsala* where you can also do some birdwatching. *Daily 9am–8pm | entrance fee 5 euros, children free | Paceco, Contrada Nubia | www.wwfsalineditrapani.it*

Let your dreams fly high: Sicily's child-friendly beaches and the deep-blue sea

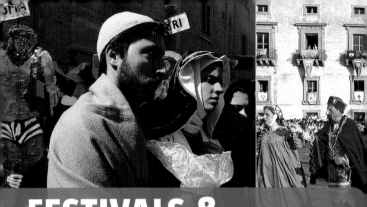

FESTIVALS & EVENTS

Most Sicilian festivals have a religious origin. The most important annual event is Holy Week, the *settimana santa*. Other highlights include *Assumption* and *carnevale*, celebrated virtually everywhere on the island.

PUBLIC HOLIDAYS

1 Jan New Year's Day, **6 Jan** Epiphany, **Easter Monday**, **25 April** Anniversary of the Liberation from Fascism, **1 May** International Workers' Day, **2 June** Founding of the Republic, **15 August** Assumption Day, **1 Nov** All Saints' Day, **8 Dec** Immaculate Conception, **25 Dec** Christmas; **26 Dec** Santo Stefano

FESTIVALS & EVENTS

3–5 FEBRUARY
▶ *Sant'Agata* – feast of the patron saint of Catania

MID FEBRUARY
▶ *Almond blossom festival* in Agrigento in the Valle dei Templi

FEBRUARY/MARCH
▶ *Carnival processions* in Sciacca and Acireale with masks and carts

MAUNDY THURSDAY
▶ *Veronica procession* in Marsala

GOOD FRIDAY
▶ *Procession of penitents* in Trapani – with hundreds of hooded men
▶ **INSIDER TIP** *I Giudei* in San Fratello

EASTER
▶ *The Dance of the Devils* in Prizzi – to chase out the winter
▶ *Albanian processions and dances* in Piana degli Albanesi

15 MAY–30 JUNE
▶ *Greek Theatre Festival* in Syrakuse – performances of ancient tragedies where they were once performed 2500 years ago

JUNE–SEPTEMBER
▶ *Orestiadi* in Gibellina – summer festival with art, music and plays

The Dance of the Devils and carnival festivities: the Sicilians celebrate religious festivals with abandon – and lots of colour, noise and fun

MID JUNE
▶ *Taormina Estate* – summer festival in amphitheatre with classical performances and concerts
▶ *Spettacoli Classici* – ancient play performed in the amphitheatre in Segesta

10–15 JUNE
▶ *Sant'Alfio* in Trecastagni – folklore and parade of Sicilian carts

27–29 JUNE
▶ *San Paolo e San Sebastiano* in Palazzolo Acreide – the saints' procession turns into a confetti battle

11–15 JULY
▶ *U Fistinu* in Palermo – festival of the patron saint, Santa Roalia, with decorated carts, processions, street markets and concerts

14 AUGUST
▶ *Palio dei Normanni* in Piazza Armerina – medieval tournament

14–15 AUGUST
▶ *Mata and Grifone* in Messina – with huge figures celebrating the liberation of Sicily from the Arabs

END OF AUGUST
▶ *Ballo della Cordella* in Petralia Sottana – harvest festival dance in local costume

END OF SEPTEMBER
INSIDER TIP ▶ *Couscous festival* in San Vito Lo Capo with chefs and recipes from Sicily, the Orient and North Africa. *www.cous cousfest.it*

13 DECEMBER
▶ *Santa Lucia* in Syracuse – festival of light

LINKS, BLOGS, APPS & MORE

LINKS

▶ www.italia.it/en/discover-italy/sicily.html The Italian Tourism official website providing all sorts of information about what to see, what to do and what to eat, with a picture gallery and personal tips

▶ www.regione.sicilia.it/beniculturali/dirbenicult/musei/museivirtualtour.html Visit more than 20 museums and excavation sites, some have virtual tours that are useful when planning a visit to such huge sites as the Valley of the Temples in Agrigento, for example. Photos, site plans, information in Italian only

▶ travel.nationalgeographic.com/travel/countries/sicily-italy-photos A visual and aesthetic album of atmospheric photographs from the *National Geographic*. Each with an informative caption giving an intimate glimpse of life on the island of Sicily

▶ www.cucinario.it Eating and drinking in Palermo and the whole of Sicily, as well as other regions in Italy. Mouth-watering photos, information in Italian only. Lots of Sicilian recipes that really make you want to get to work in the kitchen – or book a flight to Sicily

BLOGS & FORUMS

▶ www.sicily-blog.com Compiled by a wide community of Sicilian people all around the world communicating via websites, newsletters, Facebook, twitter and blogs, this site contains lots of interesting entries with photos and videos, as well as an archive

▶ www.bestofsicilyblog.com Contains news, reports and tips as well as comments,

Regardless of whether you are still preparing your trip or already in Sicily: these addresses will provide you with more information, videos and networks to make your holiday even more enjoyable

BLOGS & FORUMS

observations and opinions about Sicilian travel, culture, art, archaeology, history, sightseeing, food and wine ... all things Sicilian in fact

▶ http://sicilyguide.com The island's travel guide with information including updated news, hotels, maps, photos, videos, facts, food, the Sicily blog, multimedia, etc.

VIDEOS, STREAMS & PODCASTS

▶ www.youtube.com/watch?v=3Sum 27UCIpA&feature=related Colourful masquerade on INSIDER TIP Good Friday in San Fratello where the 'Red Devils' interrupt the festive procession

▶ www.youtube.com/watch?v=wYq-BtZAYUg&NR=1 Video diary by Sara and Ees. Four entertaining clips follow them around Palermo, from their weird hotel to discussions about the Mafia over a meal. They fiinish off with a tango evening before leaving Palermo behind them

▶ www.youtube.com/watch?v=Gpa2GfJf-j8 Stromboli is one of Italy's three active volcanoes. This short film invites you to witness one of the frequent volcanic eruptions and gives a few other impressions of the island

APPS

▶ Sicilian Dictionary Amaze the locals with your grasp of the local dialect. This app translator comes up with the appropriate phrase for everyday situations, declarations of love and insults in the Sicilian vernacular

▶ Sicily Beaches The best (or nearest) beaches on the island, listed logically, well illustrated. A must for sun worshippers

▶ Ricette siciliani collana *Pasta alla norma* and *cassata* to make at home: Sicilian recipes including a list of ingredients and degrees of difficulty, in Italian/English/French

TRAVEL TIPS

ARRIVAL

🚗 Driving down through Italy can take time, especially as the Salerno–Reggio di Calabria motorway is partially or completely closed for construction work at present with diversions along narrow, twisty mountain roads. Alternatives are the ferries from Genoa/Livorno–Palermo and Naples–Palermo. Prices, timetables and reservations under *www.traghetti.com*

🚆 Travelling by train from the UK involves several changes – in Italy, either in Milan or Rome. There are no direct lines through Europe. The cost of a sleeper and supplements for Inter City trains usually make the journey more expensive than flying. *www.trenitalia.it*

✈ A number of different airlines fly from the UK and Ireland directly to Sicily (usually Palermo or Catania). These include British Airways, Ryanair, easyJet, BMI Baby,

Thomson and Aer Lingus. Sicily is also well connected to many airports on the Italian mainland with Alitalia. Many airlines fly only a few times a week (if at all) in the low season and daily from March onwards. BA, for example, flies from London Gatwick to Catania daily from March and 3 times a week (Fri/Sat/Sun) at other times of the year. Aer Lingus flies twice a week from Dublin from the end of March to the end of October. Many airlines offer flights from the USA and Canada to Palermo and Catania via Rome, Milan or other major European cities. Direct buses run from the airport in Catania *(www.aeroporto.catania. it)* to Messina, Taormina, Ragusa, Enna, Cefalù, Agrigento and Syracuse; from Palermo airport *(www.gesap.it, www. aeroportopalermo.net)* to Trapani *(www. aeroportotrapani.com)*.

CAMPING

There are around 100 campsites on Sicily and the nearby islands. Most are on the sea and are open between Easter and the end of Oct *(www.camping.it)*. In addition, there are hundreds of places for staying overnight in your motorhome, e.g. carparks at beaches that are often free but have no facilities. There are also a few sites for motorhomes with washing facilities, roofs for shade and trees. Information under *www.camper.netsurf.it/sosta_visualizza. asp?reg=Sicilia* (in Italian only)

CAR HIRE

Major car rental companies can be found in Palermo, Catania, Syracuse, Messina, Taormina and at the airports. Prices are from around 185 euros per week if book

RESPONSIBLE TRAVEL

It doesn't take a lot to be environmentally friendly whilst travelling. Don't just think about your carbon footprint whilst flying to and from your holiday destination but also about how you can protect nature and culture abroad. As a tourist it is especially important to respect nature, look out for local products, cycle instead of driving, save water and much more. If you would like to find out more about eco-tourism please visit: *www.ecotourism.org*

From arrival to weather

Holiday from start to finish: the most important addresses and information for your trip to Sicily

on the Internet outside Italy. Booking locally costs around 25% more.

CUSTOMS

There are no longer any allowance restrictions for EU citizens on tax-free items. If you are arriving from a non-EU country, different regulations apply. Check the Internet before leaving home. For tax and duty on goods brought to the UK see: *www.hmrc. gov.uk/customs/arriving/arrivingeu.htm*

DRIVING

The maximum speed in built-up areas is 50km/h (30mph), on main roads 90km/h (55mph), on dual carriageways 110km/h (66mph), and 130km/h (80mph) on motorways (110km/h/66mph by rain; 50km/h/30mph by fog). Seatbelts must be worn in the front. It is mandatory to drive with dipped headlights outside built-up areas during the day. There must be an emergency jacket for each passenger in the car – inside the car, not in the boot! It is recommended taking a Green Card insurance document with you. The blood alcohol concentration limit is 0.5mg/alcohol per 100 ml/blood. If you get caught, you'll pay for all those who slip through the net. Speeding offences of more than 40km/h (25mph) and drunken driving (more than 1.5mg/alcohol per 100ml/blood) will cost you between 1500–6000 euros, your licence and the car that is then auctioned off. This also applies to non-Italians and for hire cars too!

In many places, no-parking zones are only marked with coloured lines on the edge of the pavement. No markings means unrestricted parking, unless signs tell you something else; yellow means reserved for the police, the *carabinieri* and local buses; black and yellow means no parking; blue means pay-and-display. Tickets can usually be bought in bars, shops, kiosks. You have to scratch the respective fields to show the time and date.

ELECTRICITY

220 Volts. Only flat pin plugs fit, otherwise an adapter is needed. International plug adapters are often not compatible!

CURRENCY CONVERTER

£	€	€	£
1	1.20	1	0.85
3	3.60	3	2.55
5	6	5	4.25
13	15.60	13	11
40	48	40	34
75	90	75	64
120	144	120	100
250	300	250	210
500	600	500	425

$	€	€	$
1	0.75	1	1.30
3	2.30	3	3.90
5	3.80	5	6.50
13	10	13	17
40	30	40	50
75	55	75	97
120	90	120	155
250	185	250	325
500	370	500	650

For current exchange rates see www.xe.com

Typically Sicilian: ceramics, flowers and muted colours

EMBASSIES & CONSULATES

BRITISH CONSULATE
Via dei Mille, 40 | 80121 Napoli NA | tel: 08 14 23 89 11 (out of office hours emergencies only: 06 42 20 00 01) | ukinitaly.fco.gov.uk/en/about-us/other-locations-in-italy/naples

US CONSULAR AGENCY
Via Vaccarini | 90143 Palermo | tel: 091 30 58 57 | naples.usconsulate.gov/about-us/regional-offices.html

EMBASSY OF CANADA
Via Zara 30 | Rome | tel. 06 854 44 39 37 | www.canada.it

EMERGENCY SERVICES

Accident/police: tel. 112 and 113 | Breakdown assistance: tel. 116 or 8 00 11 68 00 | Ambulance: tel. 118 | Fire brigade and forest fires: tel. 115 and 1515 | Coast guard: tel. 1530

ENTRANCE FEES

Most museums and historic/excavation sites cost between 3–8 euros; EU citizens under 18 or over 65 have free admission, youths between 18–25 are entitled to a 25–30 % discount. Entrance is free to many small museums. Custodians who unlock churches and palaces should be given a tip of 1–5 euros.

FARM HOLIDAYS/ AGRITOURISM

Holidaying on a farm has become a popular, low-cost and child-friendly concept throughout Italy, and gives visitors a chance to get to know an area and the people better. Agritourism on Sicily with its feudal structure often means staying in historic country houses – where the atmosphere in 'The Leopard' is brought back to life. Many farms have mountainbikes and/or horses and organise excursions. Virtually all *agriturismi* serve good country food – after all, they have to produce their own food to be certified. Information under *www.agriturismo-sicilia.it*

HEALTH

The least complicated method: in case of illness, pay for your doctor and medicine on the spot and present your bills to the health service when you return home for problem-free reimbursement. The new European Health Insurance Card (EHC) is also accepted. Emergency treatment in public hospitals is no longer entirely free of charge. X-rays and other diagnostic services incur charges which have to be paid directly to the hospital. Further information under *www.fitfortravel.nhs.uk*

HOTELS

The star categories (one for simple, five for luxury) only give a vague idea of facilities and prices. Tourist information offices have free lists with detailed descriptions of hotels, campsites and private rooms. Prices of rooms must be shown in a room or at the reception desk. One hotel search engine is: *www.regione.sicilia.it/turismo*

IMMIGRATION

Visas are not reqired for EU citizens; citizens of the US or Canada require a visa only if staying for longer than three months. Only rarely do passports need to be shown at airports, but are required when checking into hotels and campsites.

INFORMATION

ITALIAN STATE TOURIST BOARD (ENIT)
1, Princes Street | London W1B 2AY | tel. +44 20 74 08 12 54 | e-mail: info.london@ enit.it

ON SICILY
The 23 offices run by the *Servizio Turistico Regionale (STR)* can be found in 9 privincial capitals and in 14 major holiday centres. For more information see: *www.pti.regione. sicilia.it/portal/page/portal/SIT_PORTALE*. All STR offices can be contacted by e-mail: *strcefalu@regione.sicilia.it*.
Knowledge of foreign languages is rather limited. When there is no STR or other information centre, try a travel agent or the local police *(polizia municipale or vigili urbani)*, who are generally very helpful. Most hotels and guesthouses have maps and leaflets. Almost all communes have very informative websites with further links. For general information on Sicily, see: *www.regione.sicilia.it/turismo*
Information on state museums and excavation sites can also be found online: *www. regione.sicilia.it/beniculturali*. The network *www.isoladelcontemporaneo.it* includes more than 70 museums and art galleries, cultural centres, workshops, theatres and concert halls.

OPENING HOURS

Shops, supermarkets and department stores are generally open from 8.30am–1pm and 5pm–8pm. Shops close one afternoon a week – this varies however from shop to shop. During the high season, most shops in tourist areas are open all day and some well into the night. Garages are often closed on Sundays and after 8pm.

BUDGETING

Tomatoes	1–2 euros	
	for 1 kg in summer	
Coffee	min. 80 cents	
	for an espresso	
WIne	2–3 euros	
	for a carafe of wine (¼ litre)	
Petrol	1.50 euros	
	for 1 litre of super	
Parking ticket	38 euros	
	for illegal parking	
Buses in towns	1.20–1.60 euros	
	per trip	

PHONE & MOBILE PHONE

There are lots of public phones boxes. Telephone cards can be purchased in post offices and in most *tabacchi*. A local call from a public phone (3 mins) costs 10 cents; a 3-min. call abroad (to the UK) between 1.50–2 euros. If you intend phoning a lot within Italy, an Italian SIM card is worth it. These can be bought in any phone shop, even if you have no Italian tax no. *(codice fiscale)*. A photocopy of your passport is needed.
The country code for Italy is 0039. It is necessary to dial the 0 at the beginning of each fixed-line connection – both from abroad and when making local calls.

Mobile telephone numbers (often 338 or 339) are always dialled without 0. Most British mobile phones work without a problem on Sicily. You can save roaming charges by choosing the most economical network. You can avoid fees for incoming calls by using an Italian prepaid card, such as from GlobalSim *(www.globalsim.net)*. These may be expensive initially but save roaming charges. Texting is always cheap.

POST

Stamps *(francobolli)* are available from post offices and tobacconists *(tabacchi)* but hardly ever where you buy postcards. Letters and postcards by *posta prioritaria* within Italy cost 60 cents and 75 cents for elsewhere within Europe.

PRICES & CURRENCY

Sicily is not an expensive tourist destination compared to other areas in Italy. An espresso drunk standing in a bar costs less than 1 euro virtually everywhere, a glass of mineral water 50 cents, a beer or an aperitif 1.50–2 euros. In popular tourist centres, being seated and served at a table can cost two or three times as much. You must budget for between 15–30 euros for a full meal – but even if you splash out the bill will seldom be for more than 50 euros per person.

WEATHER IN CATANIA

	Jan	Feb	March	April	May	June	July	Aug	Sept	Oct	Nov	Dec
Daytime temperatures in °C/°F												
	14/57	15/59	17/63	19/66	23/73	28/82	31/88	31/88	28/82	23/73	19/66	16/61
Nighttime temperatures in °C/°F												
	8/46	8/46	9/48	12/54	15/59	19/66	22/72	23/73	20/68	16/61	13/55	9/48
Sunshine hours/day												
	4	5	6	7	8	10	11	10	8	7	6	4
Precipitation days/month												
	9	5	6	4	3	2	1	1	3	7	7	8
Water temperatures in °C/°F												
	15/59	14/57	14/57	15/59	17/63	21/70	24/75	25/77	24/75	22/72	19/66	16/61

Cash dispensers *(bancomat, postamat)* for withdrawing money with your EC card can also be found in small villages off the beaten track. Many hotels, restaurants, garages and shops take credit cards. Mastercard and Visa are widely accepted on Sicily; using your EC card with your PIN is less common.

PUBLIC TRANSPORT

Sicily's railway network is not close-knit and mostly single track. IC and express trains often run late and many stations are some way from the village or town centre. An extensive local and regional bus network, operated by a host of private companies, supplements and/or replaces the lack of a good railway system. In many towns, however, there is no central bus station. For more information see: *www.anavsicilia.it*

SMOKING

With very few exceptions, smoking is prohibited in public buildings, restaurants and bars. But as Sicilians like to have an espresso and cigarette standing, they step outside and generally accept this regulation without much complaining. Non-compliance is liable to a fine.

SUNBATHING

Carefully laid out sunbeds, such in the *stabilimenti* on the Adriatic, are more typical of the beaches around Taormina. Otherwise sunbathing on Sicily is a pretty relaxed affair and up to each individual. Nude sunbathing is not common *(www.clubnaturismo.org/italia/sicilia.html)*; topless bathing however is also popular among Sicilian women. The price of sunshades *(ombrello)* and sunbeds *(lettino, sdraio)* to rent are reasonable by Italian standards. Bartering with beach vendors is part of holidaying by the sea.

TAXI

In the large urban centres on Sicily taxis have taximeters. A tip of between 5–10% is usual. In small villages and in the countryside you are best advised to agree on a price with the driver before setting off.

TOILETS

Public WCs are few and far between and not usually in good condition. It is quite normal to drink a quick espresso before using the *bagno* in a bar – in emergency you can simply place a *mancia* of 50 cents on the bar. *Signore* is the plural of *signora*; a *signore* goes to the gents marked *Signori!*

WEATHER, WHEN TO GO

On the coast, the Mediterannean climate promises long, hot, dry summers. The best months to travel are May, June, September and October when the temperatures are pleasant, the sea warm and you miss the mass invasion of tourists in the high season and the Easter week. The winters are mild and wet. Inland and in the mountains it can be pretty chilly in summer above 1500m (5000ft) and snow falls in winter. *www.tempoitalia.it*

WOMEN TRAVELLING SOLO

Until recently, women travelling solo were considered fair game. But even Sicily has entered the modern age, things have become more relaxed and the beach *papagalli* less persistent. Hosts of compliments and flirting however are still very much part of everyday life. It is not necessarily a good idea for women travelling alone to hitch-hike.

USEFUL PHRASES ITALIAN

PRONUNCIATION

c, cc	before e or i like ch in "church", e.g. ciabatta, otherwise like k
ch, cch	like k, e.g. pacchi, che
g, gg	before e or i like j in "just", e.g. gente, otherwise like g in "get"
gl	like "lli" in "million", e.g. figlio
gn	as in "cognac", e.g. bagno
sc	before e or i like sh, e.g. uscita
sch	like sk in "skill", e.g. Ischia
z	at the beginning of a word like dz in "adze", otherwise like ts

An accent on an Italian word shows that the stress is on the last syllable.
In other cases we have shown which syllable is stressed by placing a dot below
the relevant vowel.

IN BRIEF

Yes/No/Maybe	Sì/No/Forse
Please/Thank you	Per favore/Grazie
Excuse me, please!	Scusa!/Mi scusi
May I ...?/Pardon?	Posso ...? / Come dice?/Prego?
I would like to .../Have you got ...?	Vorrei .../Avete ...?
How much is ...?	Quanto costa ...?
I (don't) like that	(Non) mi piace
good/bad	buono/cattivo/bene/male
broken/doesn't work	guasto/non funziona
too much/much/little/all/nothing	troppo/molto/poco/ tutto/niente
Help!/Attention!/Caution!	aiuto!/attenzione!/prudenza!
ambulance/police/fire brigade	ambulanza/polizia/vigili del fuoco
Prohibition/forbidden/danger/dangerous	divieto/vietato/pericolo/pericoloso
May I take a photo here/of you?	Posso fotografar La?

GREETINGS, FAREWELL

Good morning!/afternoon!/	Buon giorno!/Buon giorno!/
evening!/night!	Buona sera!/Buona notte!
Hello! / Goodbye!/See you	Ciao!/Salve! / Arrivederci!/Ciao!
My name is ...	Mi chiamo ...
What's your name?	Come si chiama?/Come ti chiami
I'm from ...	Vengo da ...

Parli italiano?

"Do you speak Italian?" This guide will help you to say the basic words and phrases in Italian.

DATE & TIME

Monday/Tuesday/Wednesday	lunedì/martedì/mercoledì
Thursday/Friday/Saturday	giovedì/venerdì/sabato
Sunday/holiday/ working day	domenica/(giorno) festivo/ (giorno) feriale
today/tomorrow/yesterday	oggi/domani/ieri
hour/minute	ora/minuto
day/night/week/month/year	giorno/notte/settimana/mese/anno
What time is it?	Che ora è? Che ore sono?
It's three o'clock/It's half past three	Sono le tre/Sono le tre e mezza
a quarter to four	le quattro meno un quarto/ un quarto alle quattro

TRAVEL

open/closed	aperto/chiuso
entrance/exit	entrata/uscita
departure/arrival	partenza/arrivo
toilets/ladies/gentlemen	bagno/toilette/signore/signori
(no) drinking water	acqua (non) potabile
Where is ...?/Where are ...?	Dov'è ...?/Dove sono ...?
left/right/straight ahead/back	sinistra/destra/dritto/indietro
close/far	vicino/lontano
bus/tram	bus/tram
taxi/cab	taxi/tassì
bus stop/cab stand	fermata/posteggio taxi
parking lot/parking garage	parcheggio/parcheggio coperto
street map/map	pianta/mappa
train station/harbour	stazione/porto
airport	aeroporto
schedule/ticket	orario/biglietto
supplement	supplemento
single/return	solo andata/andata e ritorno
train/track	treno/binario
platform	banchina/binario
I would like to rent ...	Vorrei noleggiare ...
a car/a bicycle	una macchina/una bicicletta
a boat	una barca
petrol/gas station	distributore/stazione di servizio
petrol/gas / diesel	benzina/diesel/gasolio
breakdown/repair shop	guasto/officina

FOOD & DRINK

Could you please book a table for tonight for four?	Vorrei prenotare per stasera un tavolo per quattro?
on the terrace/by the window	sulla terrazza/ vicino alla finestra
The menu, please	La carta/il menù, per favore
Could I please have ...?	Potrei avere ...?
bottle/carafe/glass	bottiglia/caraffa/bicchiere
knife/fork/spoon/salt/pepper	coltello/forchetta/cucchiaio/sale/pepe
sugar/vinegar/oil/milk/cream/lemon	zucchero/aceto/olio/latte/panna/limone
cold/too salty/not cooked	freddo/troppo salato/non cotto
with/without ice/sparkling	con/senza ghiaccio/gas
vegetarian/allergy	vegetariano/vegetariana/allergia
May I have the bill, please?	Vorrei pagare/Il conto, per favore
bill/tip	conto/mancia

SHOPPING

Where can I find...?	Dove posso trovare ...?
I'd like .../I'm looking for ...	Vorrei .../Cerco ...
Do you put photos onto CD?	Vorrei masterizzare delle foto su CD?
pharmacy/shopping centre/kiosk	farmacia/centro commerciale/edicola
department store/supermarket	grandemagazzino/supermercato
baker/market/grocery	forno/ mercato/negozio alimentare
photographic items/newspaper shop/	articoli per foto/giornalaio
100 grammes/1 kilo	un etto/un chilo
expensive/cheap/price/more/less	caro/economico/prezzo/di più/di meno
organically grown	di agricoltura biologica

ACCOMMODATION

I have booked a room	Ho prenotato una camera
Do you have any ... left?	Avete ancora ...
single room/double room	una (camera) singola/doppia
breakfast/half board/	prima colazione/mezza pensione/
full board (American plan)	pensione completa
at the front/seafront/lakefront	con vista/con vista sul mare/lago
shower/sit-down bath/balcony/terrace	doccia/bagno/balcone/terrazza
key/room card	chiave/scheda magnetica
luggage/suitcase/bag	bagaglio/valigia/borsa

BANKS, MONEY & CREDIT CARDS

bank/ATM/pin code	banca/bancomat/ codice segreto
cash/credit card	in contanti/carta di credito
bill/coin/change	banconota/moneta/il resto

USEFUL PHRASES

HEALTH

doctor/dentist/paediatrician	medico/dentista/pediatra
hospital/emergency clinic	ospedale/pronto soccorso/guardia medica
fever/pain/inflamed/injured	febbre/dolori/infiammato/ferito
diarrhoea/nausea/sunburn	diarrea/nausea/scottatura solare
plaster/bandage/ointment/cream	cerotto/fasciatura/pomata/crema
pain reliever/tablet/suppository	antidolorifico/compressa/supposta

POST, TELECOMMUNICATIONS & MEDIA

stamp/letter/postcard	francobollo/lettera/cartolina
I need a landline phone card/ I'm looking for a prepaid card for my mobile	Mi serve una scheda telefonica per la rete fissa/Cerco una scheda prepagata per il mio cellulare
Where can I find internet access?	Dove trovo un accesso internet?
dial/connection/engaged	comporre/linea/occupato
socket/adapter/charger	presa/riduttore/caricabatterie
computer/battery/rechargeable battery	computer/batteria/accumulatore
internet address (URL)/e-mail address	indirizzo internet/indirizzo email
internet connection/wifi	collegamento internet/wi-fi
e-mail/file/print	email/file/stampare

LEISURE, SPORTS & BEACH

beach/bathing beach	spiaggia/bagno/stabilimento balneare
sunshade/lounger/cable car/chair lift	ombrellone/sdraio/funivia/seggiovia
(rescue) hut/avalanche	rifugio/valanga

NUMBERS

0	zero	15	quindici
1	uno	16	sedici
2	due	17	diciassette
3	tre	18	diciotto
4	quattro	19	diciannove
5	cinque	20	venti
6	sei	21	ventuno
7	sette	50	cinquanta
8	otto	100	cento
9	nove	200	duecento
10	dieci	1000	mille
11	undici	2000	duemila
12	dodici	10000	diecimila
13	tredici	½	un mezzo
14	quattordici	¼	un quarto

NOTES

FOR YOUR NEXT HOLIDAY ...

MARCO POLO TRAVEL GUIDES

ALGARVE
AMSTERDAM
ATHENS
AUSTRALIA
AUSTRIA
BANGKOK
BARCELONA
BERLIN
BRAZIL
BRUGES, GHENT &
  ANTWERP
BRUSSELS
BUDAPEST
BULGARIA
CALIFORNIA
CAMBODIA
CANADA EAST
CANADA WEST
  ROCKIES
CAPE TOWN
  WINE LANDS,
  GARDEN ROUTE
CAPE VERDE
CHANNEL ISLANDS
CHICAGO
  & THE LAKES
CHINA
COLOGNE
COPENHAGEN
CORFU
COSTA BLANCA
  VALENCIA
COSTA BRAVA
  BARCELONA
COSTA DEL SOL
  GRANADA
CRETE
CUBA
CYPRUS
  NORTH AND
  SOUTH
DUBAI
DUBLIN
DUBROVNIK &
  DALMATIAN COAST
EDINBURGH

EGYPT
EGYPT'S RED
  SEA RESORTS
FINLAND
FLORENCE
FLORIDA
FRENCH ATLANTIC
  COAST
FRENCH RIVIERA
  NICE, CANNES &
  MONACO
FUERTEVENTURA
GRAN CANARIA
GREECE
HAMBURG
HONG KONG
  MACAU
ICELAND
INDIA
INDIA SOUTH
  GOA & KERALA
IRELAND
ISRAEL
ISTANBUL
ITALY
JORDAN
KOS
KRAKOW
LAKE GARDA

LANZAROTE
LAS VEGAS
LISBON
LONDON
LOS ANGELES
MADEIRA
  PORTO SANTO
MADRID
MALLORCA
MALTA
  GOZO
MAURITIUS
MENORCA
MILAN
MOROCCO
MUNICH
NAPLES &
  THE AMALFI COAST
NEW YORK
NEW ZEALAND
NORWAY
OSLO
PARIS
PHUKET
PORTUGAL
PRAGUE

RHODES
ROME
SAN FRANCISCO
SARDINIA
SCOTLAND
SEYCHELLES
SHANGHAI
SICILY
SINGAPORE
SOUTH AFRICA
STOCKHOLM
SWITZERLAND
TENERIFE
THAILAND
TURKEY
TURKEY
  SOUTH COAST
TUSCANY
UNITED ARAB
  EMIRATES
USA SOUTHWEST
VENICE
VIENNA
VIETNAM

- PACKED WITH INSIDER TIPS
- BEST WALKS AND TOURS
- FULL-COLOUR PULL-OUT MAP
  AND STREET ATLAS

ROAD ATLAS

The green line ▬▬ indicates the Trips & tours (p. 96–101)
The blue line ▬▬ indicates the Perfect route (p. 30–31)

All tours are also marked on the pull-out map

Photo: 'Temple E' in Selinunte

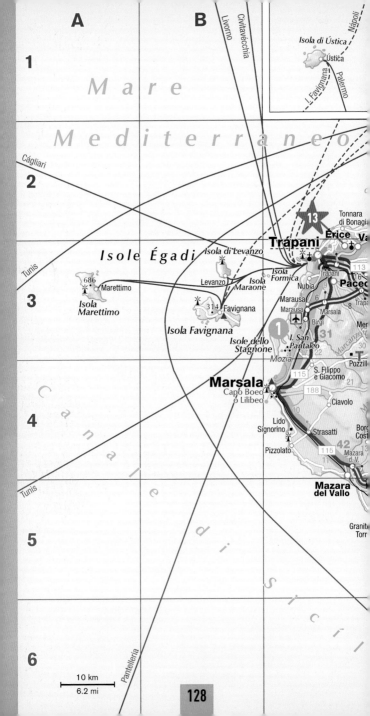

A   B

1

M a r e

Isola di Ústica
Ústica
I. Favignana

Civitavécchia
Livorno
Nápoli
Palermo

M e d i t e r r a n e o

2

Cágliari

Tunis

Isole Égadi
Isola di Levanzo

Trapani
13
Tonnara di Bonagia
Erice Va

686
Marettimo

Levanzo
Isola Maraone
Isola Formica
Isola

Nubia
Paced
113
Trapani
6

3

Isola Marettimo

314 Favignana
Isola Favignana

Isole dello Stagnone
Mozia

Marausa
Marausa
Marsala
Birgi
31
Mer
Trapa
8
6

1
I. San Pantaleo
S. Filippo e Giacomo
22
30
Pozzill
Marcanzer

Marsala
Capo Boeo o Lilibeo
115
188
Ciavolo
21

4

C a n a l e

Lido Signorino

Strasatti

42
115
11
Mazara d. V.
Borc
Cost

Pizzolato

Mazara del Vallo

5

Tunis

d i

S i c i l i

Granit
Torr

6

10 km
6.2 mi

Pantelleria

128

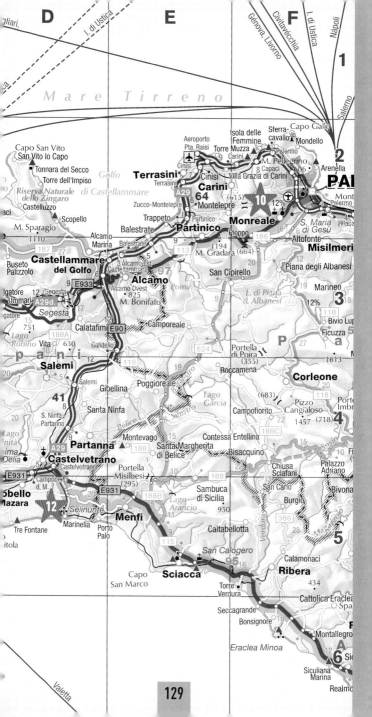

D | **E** | **F**

Génova, Livorno | I. di Ustica | Civitavecchia | Napoli

I. di Ustica

1

Mare Tirreno

Salerno

Capo San Vito
San Vito lo Capo
Tonnara del Secco
Torre dell'Impiso

Golfo

Isola delle Femmine
Sferra-cavallo
Mondello
Capo Gallo

2

Aeroporto Pta. Raisi
Torre Muzza
Carini
9
Palermo
M. Pellegrino
606
Arenella

Riserva Naturale dello Zingaro
Castelluzzo
Scopello

di Castellammare

Terrasini
Terrasini
Cinisi
Cinisi
A29
Villa Grazia di Carini

Carini
64

PAl
Mont
Palermo

M. Sparagio
1110

Zucco-Montelepre
Montelepre
(615)
10
12%

S. Maria di Gesù
Villaba

Trappeto
Balestrate
Partinico
Partinico
97
Monreale
Pioppo
186
161

Altofonte
Misilmeri

Alcamo Marina
Balestrate
9
113
M. Gradara (664)
M. 1194

Piana degli Albanesi
12

Castellammare
del Golfo
3 Alcamo Est
Castellammare
Alcamo
Alcamo Ovest
M. Bonifato 825

San Cipirello

19
Marineo

12%
3

Buseto Palizzolo

E933
Poma
9

L. di Piana d. Albanesi

118
Bivio Lu
Ficuzza
a
5

Igatore 12 (Segesta)
Ummari
A29d.
gatore 15
751
Segesta
E90
Calatafimi
12
Galitello
Camporeale
624
Portella di Poira (355)
27
P
1613

Lago Rubino
Vita 630

Salemi
Salemi
12
119
19

Roccamena

Corleone
20
118

41

Gibellina
Poggioreale
Lago Garcia

(683)
Pizzo Cangialoso
1457 (718)
Porte Imbr

20
S. Ninfa-Partanna
Santa Ninfa

Campofiorito
22
4

Lago nita Delia

Partanna
Montevago
15
188
Santa Margherita di Belice
Contessa Entellina
188C
15
10 Fi
Palazzo Adriano

A29
Castelvetrano
Castelvetrano
57
Campobello d. M.
Portella Misilbesi (295)
Bisacquino
Chiusa Sclafani
San Carlo
Bivona

E931
obello
Mazara
12

E931
188B
Sambuca di Sicilia
950
Lago Arancio
11
San Carlo
Burgio
386

Tre Fontane
Marinella
Selinunte
Porto Palo
Menfi
9

Caltabellotta
28
5

Capo San Marco
Sciacca
115
San Calogero
95 16

Calamonaci
Ribera
434

Cattolica Eracle
Spa

Torre Verdura
Seccagrande
Bonsignore
16
Montallegro
A
12
6
Si

Eraclea Minoa
Siculiana Marina
Realmo

Valetta

129

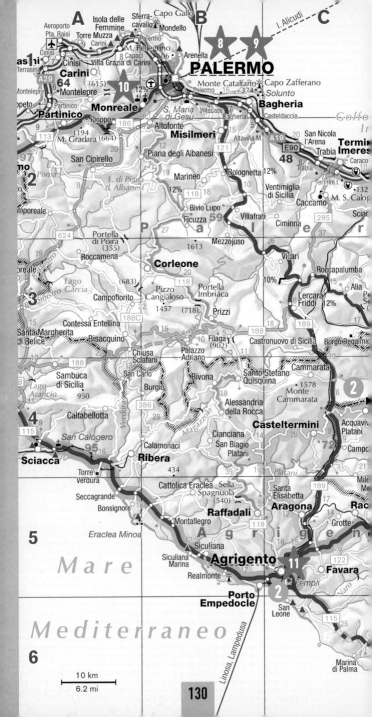

Stròmboli

Isola Strombolicchio
i Nápoli
924 Stròmboli
i Vàncori

Isola di Basiluzzo

Isola Lisca Bianca
Pietro

Nápoli, Génova, Civitavecchia

Salerno

Capo Vaticano

Golfo

di Gioia

Jo

Nic

San F

Lido di Palm

Palmi

Bagnara
Calabra

Costa Viola

A3

ano

Capo
di Milazzo
Paradiso

Golfo di Milazzo

S. Saba

Spartà

Torre Faro

Scilla

Villa S. Giovanni
Campo Calabro

Villafranca Tirrena
Rometta

Villafranca T.

Castanea
delle Furie
609

Sant'Agata

Milazzo

Spadafora

Villafranca T.

E90

15

20

Scilla

Divieto

Milazzo

Santa Marina

Milazzo-I.Eólie

113

Olivarella

18

Saponara

Messina
Centro

Rometta

Gallico

Villa
San Giovanni

Calanna

Barcellona

A20

Monforte
San Giorgio

1127

MESSINA

Santo Stefano
in Aspromonte

fo
atti

20

cone

Barcellona
P. di Gotto

Santa Lucia
del Mela

Mess.Sud-
Tremestieri

Galati
Marina

Calopinace

Sant'Agata

iari

185

Castroreale

Monte
Poverello
1279

26

RÉGGIO
DI CALABRIA

Cardeto

P

13

Ro
Gre

Novara
di Sicilia

1288

Italia

88

San-Gregorio 1051
M. Embrisi

Ba

340

Fondachelli Fântina

Fiumedinisi

A18

Scaletta
Zanclea

Péllaro

E90

Motta
San Giovanni

la
usa

27

Antillo

Mandanici

E45

Ali Terme

Roccalumera

Bocale

Montebello
Iónico

Montagna
Grande

Casalvecchio
Sículo
S. Teresa di R

Savoca

114

Roccalumera

Lazzaro

30

15

1374

Forza d'Agrò

14

Santa Teresa di Riva

Francavilla di Sicília
Melia

185

Mar
San

iaro

22

Taormina

Letojanni

Melito
di Porto Salvo

Linguaglossa

13

Gaggi

Giard.-Naxos

Taormina

Mare

Calatabiano

Giardini-Naxos

Iónio

areneve

15

Fiumefreddo

Fiumefreddo di Sicília

Ili

Sant

A18

23

Mascali

Alfio

8

Milo

Riposto

Giarre

Giarre

6

Santa

Pozzillo

135

Monti Peloritani

Mare

Stretto di Messina

di Gioia

10 km
6.2 mi

KEY TO ROAD ATLAS

Motorway with junctions	Autobahn mit Anschlussstellen
Motorway under construction	Autobahn in Bau
Toll station	Mautstelle
Roadside restaurant and hotel	Raststätte mit Übernachtung
Roadside restaurant	Raststätte
Filling-station	Tankstelle
Dual carriage-way with motorway characteristics with junction	Autobahnähnliche Schnellstraße mit Anschlussstelle
Trunk road	Fernverkehrsstraße
Thoroughfare	Durchgangsstraße
Important main road	Wichtige Hauptstraße
Main road	Hauptstraße
Secondary road	Nebenstraße
Railway	Eisenbahn
Car-loading terminal	Autozug-Terminal
Mountain railway	Zahnradbahn
Aerial cableway	Kabinenschwebebahn
Railway ferry	Eisenbahnfähre
Car ferry	Autofähre
Shipping route	Schifffahrtslinie
Route with beautiful scenery	Landschaftlich besonders schöne Strecke
Alleenstr. Tourist route	Touristenstraße
XI-V Closure in winter	Wintersperre
Road closed to motor traffic	Straße für Kfz gesperrt
8% Important gradients	Bedeutende Steigungen
Not recommended for caravans	Für Wohnwagen nicht empfehlenswert
Closed for caravans	Für Wohnwagen gesperrt
Important panoramic view	Besonders schöner Ausblick

Wartenstein *Umbalfälle* Of interest: culture - nature	Sehenswert: Kultur - Natur
Bathing beach	Badestrand
National park, nature park	Nationalpark, Naturpark
Prohibited area	Sperrgebiet
Church	Kirche
Monastery	Kloster
Palace, castle	Schloss, Burg
Mosque	Moschee
Ruins	Ruinen
Lighthouse	Leuchtturm
Tower	Turm
Cave	Höhle
Archaeological excavation	Ausgrabungsstätte
Youth hostel	Jugendherberge
Isolated hotel	Allein stehendes Hotel
Refuge	Berghütte
Camping site	Campingplatz
Airport	Flughafen
Regional airport	Regionalflughafen
Airfield	Flugplatz
National boundary	Staatsgrenze
Administrative boundary	Verwaltungsgrenze
Check-point	Grenzkontrollstelle
Check-point with restrictions	Grenzkontrollstelle mit Beschränkung
ROMA Capital	Hauptstadt
VENÉZIA Seat of the administration	Verwaltungssitz
Trips & tours	Ausflüge & Touren
Perfect route	Perfekte Route
MARCO POLO Highlight	

INDEX

This index lists all places, sights and beaches in this guide. Numbers in bold indicate a main entry.

WRITE TO US

e-mail: info@marcopologuides.co.uk

Did you have a great holiday? Is there something on your mind? Whatever it is, let us know! Whether you want to praise, alert us to errors or give us a personal tip – MARCO POLO would be pleased to hear from you. We do everything we can to provide the very latest information for your trip.

Nevertheless, despite all of our authors' thorough research, errors can creep in. MARCO POLO does not accept any liability for this. Please contact us by e-mail or post.

MARCO POLO Travel Publishing Ltd Pinewood, Chineham Business Park Crockford Lane, Chineham Basingstoke, Hampshire RG24 8AL United Kingdom

PICTURE CREDITS

Cover photograph: Taormina, Madonna della Rocca (Getty Images/Photographer's Choice: Slow Images)
Agriturismo Limoneto: Dora Moscati (17 top); DuMont Bildarchiv: Feldhoff & Martin (20, 38, 39, 48, 52, 62, 85, 110/111), Lubenow (98); Feldhoff & Martin (78); J. Frangenberg (45, 67); F. M. Frei (8); R. Freyer (28/29, 37, 41, 51, 58, 65); Getty Images/Photographer's Choice: Slow Images (1 top); R. Hackenberg (2 bottom, 3 top, 3 centre, 46/47, 57, 60/61, 72/73, 80, 96/97, 99 bottom, 105, 126/127); H. Hartmann (71); Huber: Baviera (55), Liese (front flap left, 74), Lubenow (2 top, 5, 34), Roberto (83), Saffo (12/13, 30 bottom), Simeone (10/11); Huber Images/SIME: Saffo (6, 101); Kempinski Hotel Giardino di Costanza: Adrian Huston (16 centre); M. Kirchgessner (3 bottom, 23, 24/25, 26 r., 27, 28, 29, 42/43, 69, 77, 86/87, 102/103, 110, 111, 116, 137); Laif: Barbagallo (4), Eid (99 top), Madej (113); Laif/Contrasto: Shobha (9); La Terra Magica: Lenz (front flap right, 2 centre bottom, 32/33, 88, 90, 93); mauritius images: Alamy (30 top), CuboImages (2 centre top, 7), foodcollection (26 l.); mauritius images/imagebroker: Bahnmüller (18/19); Orient Photo (15); Paradise Beach Club (16 bottom); Peter Peter (1 bottom); Carmelina Ricciardello (16 top); The Rocco Forte Collection (17 bottom); T. Stankiewicz (95, 109); vario images: Baumgarten (106/107)

1st Edition 2012
Worldwide Distribution: Marco Polo Travel Publishing Ltd, Pinewood, Chineham Business Park, Crockford Lane, Basingstoke, Hampshire RG24 8AL, United Kingdom. Email: sales@marcopolouk.com
© MAIRDUMONT GmbH & Co. KG, Ostfildern
Chief editor: Marion Zorn
Author: Hans Bausenhardt, co-author: Peter Peter, editor: Christina Sothmann
Programme supervision: Ann-Katrin Kutzner, Nikolai Michaelis, Silwen Randebrock
Picture editor: Stefan Scholtz, Gabriele Forst
What's hot: wunder media, Munich
Cartography road atlas & pull-out map: © MAIRDUMONT, Ostfildern
Design: milchhof: atelier, Berlin; Front cover, pull-out map cover, page 1: factor product munich
Translated from German by Christopher Wynne; editor of the English edition: Christopher Wynne
Prepress: M. Feuerstein, Wigel
Phrase book in cooperation with Ernst Klett Sprachen GmbH, Stuttgart, Editorial by Pons Wörterbücher

DOS & DON'TS

A few things you should bear in mind when on Sicily

DON'T FALL FOR STREET TRADERS

At market stands you can pick and choose, rummage around and handle things just as the locals do. There are usually price tags or else you can just watch and see what other people pay. Where you do have to be careful is with certain 'craftsmen' who weave a web of secrecy around their goods and promise you a once-in-a-lifetime bargain. In many cases they ask you for an advance payment.

DO TRY THE LOCAL SPECIALITIES

Almost all restaurants have a set-meal – the *menú turistico* – at a price that includes two courses, a dessert, a drink, the cover charge, tax and service. Very few locals ever choose this even though it is much cheaper than eating à la carte. The food is generally pretty uninspiring and only very seldom are typical local dishes served. Instead you'll get a schnitzel, chicken or a slice of beef, a few limp lettuce leaves and half a tomato.

DON'T INVITE THIEVES

Thieves and pickpockets are not lurking on every corner but there is a greater risk in the larger cities, ports and on a number of beaches. Don't leave anything visible in a car or else you risk having the windows smashed. When driving through Palermo and Catania lock the doors and the boot. Thefts from cars on Sicily are not generally worse than anywhere else, but these two cities appear quite near the top of the statistics table for robbery and pickpocketing in Italy. This applies especially to handbag thefts from moving cars and mopeds *(scippo)*. Don't carry a handbag or shoulder bag unless you really have to, and always make sure it's on the building side of the pavement, not the road side. And, like everywhere else, pickpockets love markets and stations, bus stations and crowded streets.

DO REMEMBER
LO SCONTRINO

Always take the receipt with you even if you have only bought a bottle of water. The scontrino is proof that goods or services have been correctly booked and tax will be paid. Exceptions are petrol, cigarettes and newspapers. Plain-clothed tax fraud investigators may be within a 100m radius. If you cannot present a receipt, both you and the shopkeeper will have to pay a hefty fine.

DON'T PLAY WITH FIRE

Year for year hundreds of fires destroy woods, olive groves and gardens, and threaten houses and even whole villages. Usually only a barren stone desert is left afterwards. Cigarette ends, picnic fires, the hot exhaust of your car parked on dry grass or leaves can all have catastrophic consequences.